The NAUTI-BENDER 900
Question & Answer

SKIPPER'S CHALLENGE

SEAMANSHIP & SMALL BOAT HANDLING

Dale R. Lydigsen

ENjoy The "Challenge"!

Dale R. Lydigsen

PENCHANT PUBLISHING

Post Office Box 109

Jackson, New Hampshire 03846

www.PenchantPublishing.com

ENDORSEMENTS

SKIPPER'S CHALLENGE

PUBLISHED BY: Penchant Publishing

AUTHOR: Dale R. Lydigsen, Jr.

THIRD EDITION: 2004

ISBN: 1-893697-17-7

LIBRARY OF CONGRESS CATALOG NUMBER: 98-91659

PRINTED: In China

PURCHASE INFORMATION: For sales/ordering inquiries, special pricing or information on where to purchase Penchant Publishing's books and calendars contact our sales department at 800-235-7221 or fax 603-383-8108.

PENCHANT PUBLISHING

PHONE 603-383-4000   Post Office Box 109   FAX 603-383-8108
Jackson, New Hampshire 03846

E-mail: info@PenchantPublishing.com • www.PenchantPublishing.com

PUBLISHER'S ACKNOWLEDGEMENTS

We're proud of this book and plan to continue publishing it for many years to come. To help maintain the highest standards of quality and accuracy, we would welcome any comments you may have (good and bad).

Please write to our Editorial Department at Penchant Publishing, PO Box 109, Jackson, NH 03846.

We would also like to express our appreciation and sincere thanks to the many individuals that have contributed to this book's publication:

Technical Consultants: Captains: Vince Tibbetts, Dick Winchell, Al Stephens and Bob Williams.

Editors: Peggy Schleicher, Elizabeth Dempsey, and Janina Lamb.

Graphic Design: Virginia Howe.

Art Design: Maureen Rupp, Gayle Lemeri, Jodie Neal, Bill Nicholson and Mark Nelson.

Cover Photo Credits: Photo by Carlo Borlenghi.

Special Thanks: To the many boat manufacturers, government agencies, and individuals that contributed some of the great photography that you will enjoy in this book.

CONTENTS

CONTENTS

*'Seamanship' is having a good sense of the sea, boats and
how they react together in a rapidly changing environment.*

Every marina has its share of 'Mr. Magoos', boaters who always
seem to 'require assistance' in one form or another, whether at the
dock where their antics spawn a whole new host of nicknames like
'crash' or 'fend-off' or offshore where many well known rocks and
shoals are affectionately renamed after them.

On the other hand, every marina also has Skippers who seem to
handle identical situations with the greatest of ease. Obviously, the
difference between the Mr. Magoos and the Skippers is good seamanship. It is typically a lack or lapse of this sense that gets boaters
into trouble while on-the-water.

You're not born with good seamanship, it is acquired it through
education and experience. A Skipper's Challenge is two-fold: the
subject is complex/comprehensive at the same time the vast major-
ity of recreational boaters are on-the-water only on a part-time or
seasonal basis. It's easy for skills to get rusty.

With the above in mind, **our *Skipper's Challenge*** was developed to
help boaters shortcut the school of 'hard rocks', learn new things,
measure and most importantly **maintain** their skills. This book was
written especially for recreational boaters and emphasizes the prac-
tical day-to-day seamanship knowledge required for us to safely
enjoy our favorite pasttime.

In a final note, our thanks to the many individuals who have con-
scientiously contributed to this book. If you have any suggestions
for improvements (or locate any of our 'Mr. Magoos'), please let us
know. We enjoy hearing what our readers have to say.

- Dale R. Lydigsen

ABOUT THIS BOOK

FORMAT:

The game-like, question and answer format is offered as a fun alternative to the somewhat 'dry' reading typical of most nautical reference manuals.

SUBJECT MATTER:

"Nauti-Bender" questions range from simple to complex and are organized by subject in a random fashion like the skills needed while on-the-water. However, the handy thumb index (see back cover) and the associated tabs on each page can be utilized to re-visit more troublesome subjects.

ANSWERS:

Given the nature of this book, the format does not lend itself to lengthy explanations. For further clarification, it is suggested the reader seek out a good reference manual. Nauti-Bender answers were purposely placed on the next facing page after questions to discourage 'shortcuts over shoal waters'.

WHERE TO START:

Beginners or novices should probably review the 'language' category initially. Others can follow the book from beginning to end or category by category. It's your choice.

REVIEW:

To stay as seaworthy as your boat, we recommend that the 'Challenge' be reviewed on a regular basis.

GOOD LUCK!!

Typically, it is a lack or lapse of _____ that gets boaters in trouble while on-the-water.

PHOTO: COURTESY OF BENETEAU USA, INC.

The direction and force the wind seems to have when observed from a vessel in motion is referred to as _____ _____.

NAUTI-BENDER
Answers

*The answers to the Nauti-Benders in this book are given on the **next facing page**.*

For example, the answers for the above are given on page 4.

"_____" construction: a method of boat building in which the lower edge of each side plank overlaps the upper edge of the one below it.

A triangular, rectangular, or swallowtailed flag, usually associated with yacht club membership, is called a "_____".

PHOTO: BY JOHN SNYDER, NORTH CONWAY, NH

"Poor Man's Haul Out": Make her fast to a pier and wait for the tide to go out; or run her up on a sandy beach and when the tide falls... "_____" her over on one side or prop up on both sides.

You want to go where? When a skipper is very familiar with certain waters, he is said to have "_____ _____".

NAUTI-BENDER
Answers

*The answers to the Nauti-Benders in this book are given on the **next facing page**.*

For example, the answers for the above are given on page 5.

PHOTO: COURTESY OF TRACKER MARINE, LLC. BY: MIKE FULLER

"Safe Speed" is the speed at which you can take proper corrective action to avoid _____.

When going downstream or with a strong tidal current, it sometimes becomes difficult to control the vessel's speed and direction. What corrective measure could the skipper take?

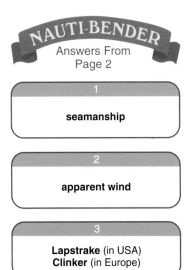

NAUTI-BENDER
Answers From
Page 2

1

seamanship

2

apparent wind

3

Lapstrake (in USA)
Clinker (in Europe)

River Cruising Rule-of-Thumb: Generally, the swiftest water is found closer to shore. Running downstream, stay in the _____ of the channel; when heading upstream, stay as close to the _____ bank as possible.

A vessel proceeding up a shallow, narrow channel may experience "bank suction". This phenomenon will force the **stern** or **bow** – **away** or **toward** the nearest bank.

A "towing bridle" is used: (A) **for more control**; (B) **to distribute the strain equally between two points vs. one;** or (C) **to reduce the amount of power required for the tow.**

When towing another vessel, the tow rope should be... **as long as possible**; **as short as possible**; or, **such that the vessels are "in-step"**.

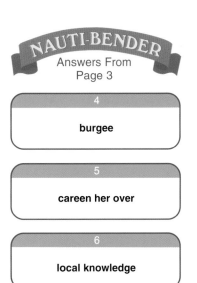

NAUTI-BENDER
Answers From
Page 3

4
burgee

5
careen her over

6
local knowledge

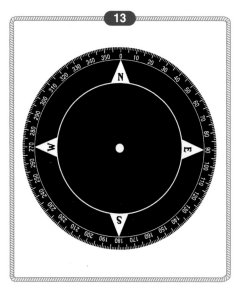

13

There are how many "points" in a mariner's circle... **18**, **32**, or **36**?

14

If you're in thick fog and wish to determine the approximate distance to shore, blow your air horn (aimed towards land) and count the seconds until the echo returns. Twelve seconds would equal approximately _____ nautical mile(s).

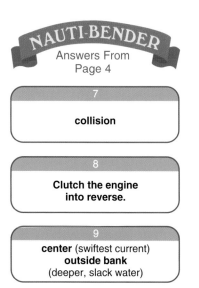

NAUTI-BENDER
Answers From Page 4

7

collision

8

Clutch the engine into reverse.

9

center (swiftest current)
outside bank
(deeper, slack water)

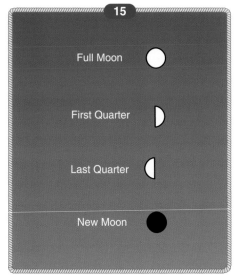

15

Full Moon ○

First Quarter ◗

Last Quarter ◖

New Moon ●

During which phase of the moon, will it be south of you at midnight (northern hemisphere)?

Basic Principles of Navigating in Fog: Keep your eyes _____; keep your ears _____; keep your _____-_____ plot; and most importantly... keep your _____!

To Navigate by the Stars: Note the position of a star (mid-sky) relative to something on the boat, wait 20 minutes... **in what direction is the star** (sighting taken from the same place), if it moved: **up**, **down**, **left** or **right**?

To determine if a light is on the horizon, move your head up and down about a foot (while watching the light). If the light disappears... **it is** or **it is not** on the horizon.

NAUTI-BENDER
Answers From
Page 5

10
stern toward the nearest bank
(increased water velocity and
suction of the prop)

11
**B: to distribute the strain
equally between two
points vs. one**

12
in-step (Tug and towboats should
reach wave crest or the trough
simultaneously.)

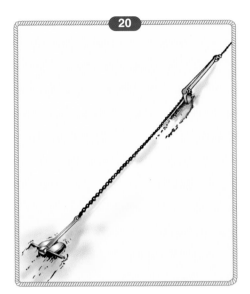

Anchoring – Final Step: The _____ should inspect the foredeck to ensure that the anchor rode is properly cleated/stowed, the required scope has been payed out and proper chafing gear has been installed.

Expecting a blow, anchors laid in "_____" can be quite effective. The adjoining chain should be taut (for maximum holding power) and should be 1½ times the water's depth for easy retrieval.

NAUTI-BENDER
Answers From
Page 6

13
32 points

14
one nautical mile (1,000 feet per second)

15
full moon

Before anchoring, what is the most important consideration: (A) **holding ground**; (B) **number, type, and position of boats present and anticipated**; (C) **anticipated winds/weather**; or (D) **water depth, current direction, tidal range**?

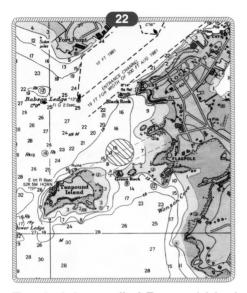

The shaded area off of Tenpound Island (shown above) would offer an excellent anchorage when the prevailing wind is **northeast** or **southwest**.

Adding a length of chain between the line and the anchor increases the anchor's holding power and reduces bottom chafe. In general, the chain should be the boat's **length** or **beam** plus _____ feet.

PHOTO: COURTESY OF THE U.S. COAST GUARD

The First Rule of Safe Anchoring: always or **never** anchor to the **leeward** or **windward** of the shore.

NAUTI-BENDER
Answers From
Page 7

16
**eyes: open; ears: open;
dead-reckoning plot;
keep your head!**

17
**if up – east; if down – west;
if left – north; if right – south**

18
it is on the horizon
(This method is called bobbing
the horizon or dipping a light.)

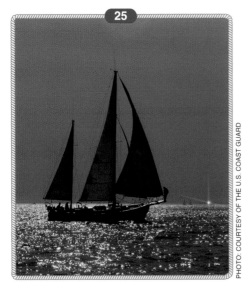

PHOTO: COURTESY OF THE U.S. COAST GUARD

25

As you approach the coast, returning from Bimini to Port Everglades, you sight the mid-channel buoy which flashes: **every five seconds**; **quick flashes**; or **Morse code for "A"**.

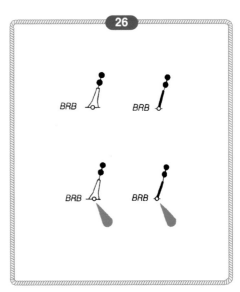

26

What do the chart symbols shown above indicate to the navigator?

27

You're lost in thick fog. All of a sudden you hear a buoy. You know it's a gong buoy because: the tone is **different** or the **same** each time you hear it.

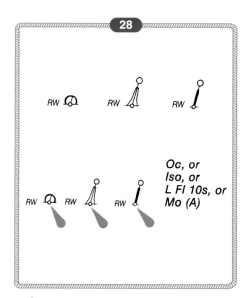

What do the chart symbols shown above indicate to the navigator?

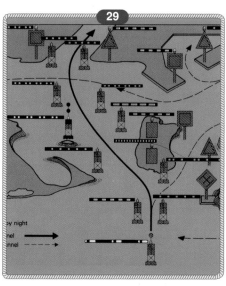

Buoy Recognition: **Quick flashing** or **occulting** buoys often indicate an area of special concern, such as sharp channel junctions or obstructions. In general, the faster the flash, the more important the buoy.

You're lost in the fog... all of a sudden you hear a buoy. You know it's a bell buoy because: the tone is the **same** or **different** each time?

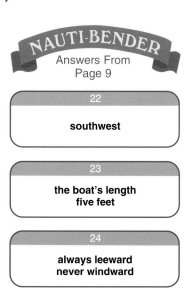

NAUTI-BENDER
Answers From
Page 9

22
southwest

23
the boat's length five feet

24
always leeward never windward

31

Remember, if everyone tries to fend off on the same side, the boat may heel and tangle her _____.

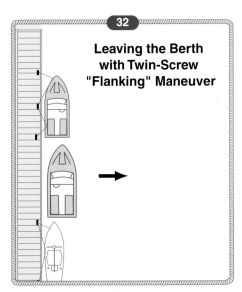

32

Leaving the Berth with Twin-Screw "Flanking" Maneuver

Position the rudders toward the dock. Shift into **reverse** or **forward** on the inboard engine and **reverse** or **forward** on the outboard engine. Adjust the throttles as necessary to clear the dock.

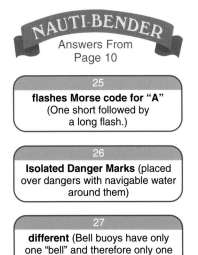

NAUTI-BENDER
Answers From Page 10

25

flashes Morse code for "A"
(One short followed by a long flash.)

26

Isolated Danger Marks (placed over dangers with navigable water around them)

27

different (Bell buoys have only one "bell" and therefore only one tone.)

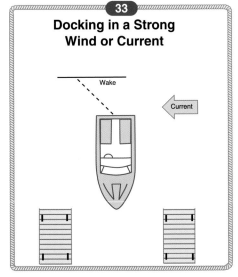

33

Docking in a Strong Wind or Current

Wake

Current

When making a straight run for the dock, watch the boat's wake in relationship to the boat's _____. The degree to which the wind/current is pushing your boat can be judged fairly well.

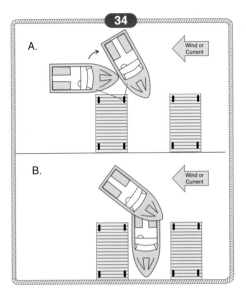

Which approach angle: "**A**" or "**B**" shown above would result in the most successful docking maneuver?

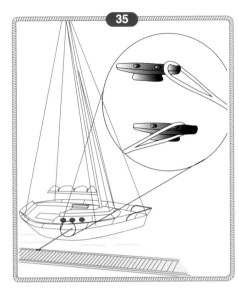

Spring line departures are made easier using the cleat quick-release technique (shown above) which will hold well under _____ yet release easily after the maneuver.

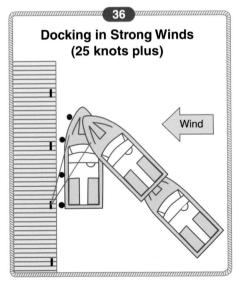

Docking in Strong Winds (25 knots plus)

Drift into the dock at a 60° – 80° angle with the rudder amidships and the engine in reverse. Secure the after spring line to the dock. Position rudder **away from** or **towards** the dock while adjusting power to keep bow from hitting the dock.

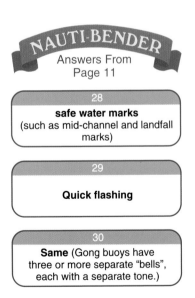

A Sheepshank knot is commonly used by lobstermen to _____ a line.

A "_____" can be used to quickly join two lines.

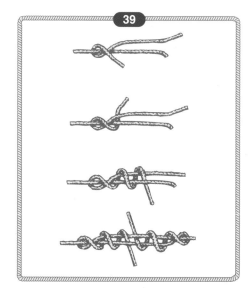

The _____ *knot* or *blood knot*, tied as shown above, is ideal to **permanently** join two lines.

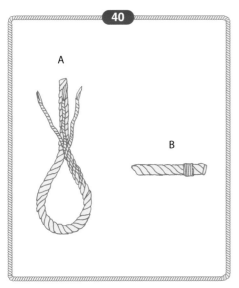

40

A

B

The way strands of a rope are wound together is referred to as the: **bend**; **twist**; **lay**; or **coil**.

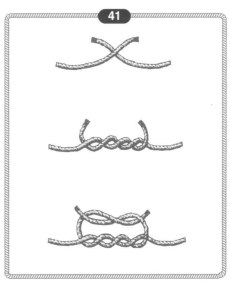

41

A "_____ knot" is useful to keep tension on items being lashed together until the final overhand loop is made.

42

To quickly make fast to a piling, use a "_____ hitch"... make a right under-handed loop, make another one, slip the second on top of the first, then slip both loops over the piling and pull tight.

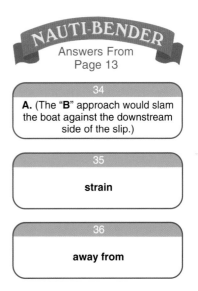

NAUTI-BENDER
Answers From
Page 13

34
A. (The "**B**" approach would slam the boat against the downstream side of the slip.)

35
strain

36
away from

PHOTO: COURTESY OF GRAND BANKS YACHTS

You're traveling on your boat along with a friend on his boat, and arrive late at a busy harbor. What is the polite way to cross the trawler that you have rafted on either side of?

PHOTO: COURTESY OF THE U.S. COAST GUARD

The Intracoastal Waterway (ICW) runs from Boston to _____ via a clearly-marked channel with depths adequate to float 100-foot barges as well as the largest private vessels.

NAUTI-BENDER
Answers From
Page 14

37

shorten

38

bowline

39

barrel knot (Note: this knot works especially well with monofilament line.)

Boat Trailering: Tongue weight should be _____ to _____ percent of the GTW (**G**ross **T**railer **W**eight – weight of trailer, boat fuel, and cargo while on the road).

Optical Illusions: From a large ship's bridge, visibility is foreshortened – vessels appear to be closer than they are. The converse applies to a small boat low in the water – **True** or **False**?

Most pleasure boats must be "registered" with the state or "documented" federally if overseas travel is intended. To be documented, a boat is generally over 30' and exceeds five _____ registered tons (a measurement of cubic volume).

NAUTI-BENDER
Answers From
Page 15

40
the *lay*

41
Ligature knot – commonly called the surgeon's knot

42
clove hitch

Preparing to start your engine for the first cruise of the year (full gas tank), you squeeze the gas line bulb. It doesn't get hard and you hear a sucking sound within the gas tank. What is the problem/solution?

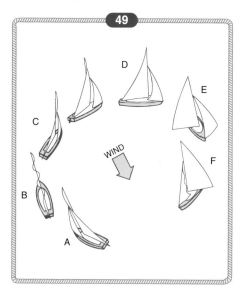

49

Typically, what is the minimum angle a close-hauled boat can "point into the wind": **35°**; **45°**; or **50°**?

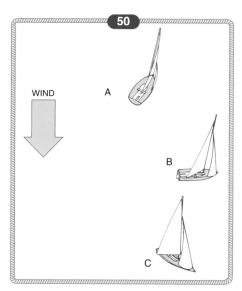

50

Apparent wind would have the greatest effect on which vessel shown above?

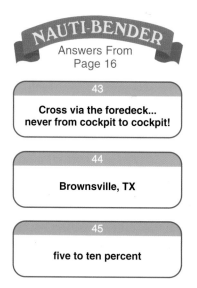

NAUTI-BENDER
Answers From
Page 16

43

Cross via the foredeck... never from cockpit to cockpit!

44

Brownsville, TX

45

five to ten percent

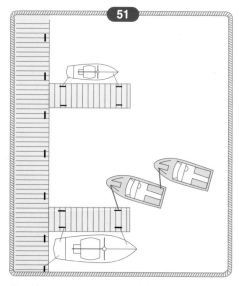

51

Docking a tow can be tricky; however, the method shown above enables the tug to push the tow ahead, or go astern to _____ her (without changing the bow line), or turn and nudge the tow's stern in with her bow.

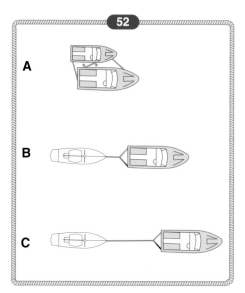

There are three basic towing configurations. Match the following with the appropriate towing method shown above): ( ) **a short tow with no obstructions**; ( ) **towing with obstructions in calm water**; and ( ) **towing at sea**.

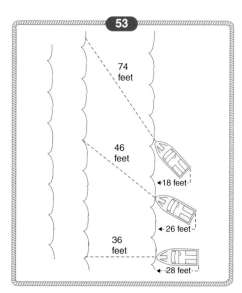

Instead of heading directly into high seas, try "angling" into them. Depending on the angle, this maneuver can increase the "wave-to-boat-length ratio" by up to _____, thus creating a more comfortable ride.

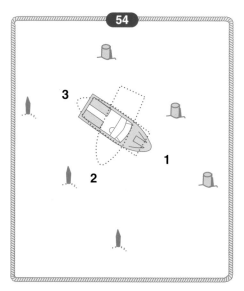

To best turn a twin-screw vessel as shown above, use: (A) **both engines ahead with right rudder**; (B) **port engine ahead only**; (C) **port engine ahead and starboard engine astern**; or (D) **both engines astern with right rudder**.

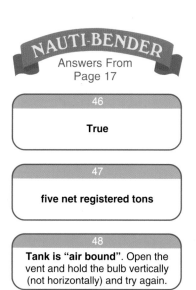

NAUTI-BENDER
Answers From
Page 17

46

True

47

five net registered tons

48

Tank is "air bound". Open the vent and hold the bulb vertically (not horizontally) and try again.

Spraying flags, burgees, ensigns, etc. with Scotch Guard™ will prolong their life (especially in salt water environments) up to: **two times**; **three times**; or **four times** normal.

Are your Lexan or Plexiglas port holes/ windshield getting cloudy? Avoid using household glass cleaners; they typically contain _____, which reacts badly to plastic.

NAUTI-BENDER
Answers From Page 18

49
45°

50
B (getting the most advantage)

51
stop her

Boat winterizing should include filling the inboard fuel tank(s) to: ¼; ½; or **F** and adding fuel stabilizer.

Rather than discharging toxic drain cleaners overboard, unclog sink drains or heads by flushing with _____ _____ followed by boiling water through the lines.

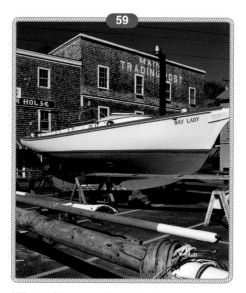

Winter Storage: Keel blocking – use wood (preferably) or cement blocks, never cinder blocks. Never use a single cement block standing on its **short** or **long** side.

Smoke from the Exhaust (gasoline engine): blue smoke is the normal color for a _____-stroke engine and indicates internal wear in a _____-stroke engine.

Answers From
Page 19

52
B: short tow, no obstructions **A:** towing with obstructions **C:** towing at sea

53
fourfold

54
C: port engine ahead and starboard engine astern

61

SAIL LANGUAGE

Luffing – The sails are not completely filled with wind, the vessel slows.

Backing down – The wind is blowing against the forward surface of the sails.

Full – The wind is blowing against the after surface of the sails.

Back and Fill – Maneuvering a vessel in confined waters by allowing the sails alternately to go aback and to go full.

In stays – The vessel is headed directly into the wind, with steerageway.

In irons – The vessel is headed directly into the wind, without steerageway.

Aback – The wind against the forward surface of the sails is pushing the vessel backwards.

Which of the above two sailing definitions have been transposed?

62

U.S. Terms	British Terms
Hose Clip	Jubilee Clip
Wire Clamp	Bulldog Grip
Lapstrake	Clinker
Wildcat	Gypsy
Boom Vang	Fairlead
Spreader	Crosstree
Chock	Kicking Strap
Head	Heads
Turnbuckle	Rigging Screw
Gunkholing	Ditchcrawling

Going sailing with our British friends... you better speak their language! Which of the two "United States" terms shown above have been transposed?

NAUTI-BENDER

Answers From Page 20

55

four times

56

ammonia

57

fuel tank(s) should be filled
(to prevent as much condensation as possible)

63

SAILBOAT OR HOUSEHOLD ITEMS?

1. "TANG"
2. "ROACH"
3. "GOOSENECK"
4. "THIMBLE"
5. "COFFEE GRINDER"
6. "DOG HOUSE"
7. "HEADBOARD"
8. "RAKE"
9. "LADDER"
10. "ROCKER"

All of the above terms could be used to describe things that maybe found **around the house**, on a **sailboat**, or **both**.

64
OLD NAVAL SLANG

"Dead Marine" – Empty liquor bottle.

"Irish Pennant" – End of a line.

"S.O.S." – Save our ship (souls).

"Hog-Yoke" – Sextant.

"Son of a gun" – Male born at sea.

"Splice the main brace" – have a drink.

"Dunnage" – Sailor's personal gear.

"Bitter end" – A frayed line.

"Scuttlebutt" – Water cask (water fountain – modern day).

Which of the above definitions have been transposed?

65
LINE HANDLING LANGUAGE
1. SLACK: feed line out.
2. TAKE UP: take slack out.
3. EASE: momentarily ease a line under strain (stopped boat).
4. HOLD: take enough turns to stop the boats.
5. CHECK: "hold" it intermittently to slow the boat.
6. SURGE: pay out line (moving boat).
7. MAKE FAST: secure the line.
8. ALL FAST: secure all lines.
9. DOUBLE UP: put on a second line.
10. SINGLE UP: take in extra lines.
11. STAND BY: be ready to tend it.
12. LET GO: cast off the line.

Which of the above line handling terms **do not** correspond with the given definitions?

66
LANGUAGE OF THE SEA

Arm: part of an anchor.

Belly: the part of a sail that bulges out from the pressure of the wind.

Breast: a docking line.

Brow: gangplank.

Chest: box containing cargo.

Eye: the end of a line.

Foot: lower edge of a sail.

Head: part of an anchor.

Palm: part of an anchor.

Rib: boat frame.

Language of the Sea: Which of the above nautical terms/definitions emanating from the human anatomy is incorrect?

Answers From
Page 21

58
baking soda

59
short side (not as strong... a single block could break... always use pairs)

60
two-stroke engine
four-stroke engine

67

Assuming you are in the power vessel shown above and you see a green light and a white light on an approaching power vessel, is it going to pass you on the **port** or **starboard side**?

PHOTO: COURTESY OF THE U.S. COAST GUARD

68

Suddenly, looming out of the fog to port, you observe the green running light of another powerboat which appears to be on a constant bearing... **what should you do next**?

NAUTI-BENDER

Answers From
Page 22

61

The "Backing down" definition
is transposed
with "Aback".

62

"chock"
has been transposed with
"boom vang"

63

both the house and boat

69

PHOTO: COURTESY OF BOSTON TOW & TRANSPORTATION

While cruising in fog, you hear a sound signal ahead (a long blast followed by three short blasts) indicating a vessel being towed and _____.

A continuous fog signal indicates a vessel in _____.

If you see a red light and a white light on an approaching vessel, it's going to pass you **starboard** or **port** side-to.

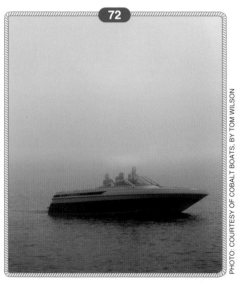

In fog, when it comes to making sound signals, boats under 12 meters (39.4 feet) **do** or **do not** have to make fog signals as set forth in the navigation rules.

Answers From
Page 23

64
The "Irish Pennant"
definition is transposed
with "Bitter End".

65
3. (ease)
should be 6. (surge)
and vice versa.

66
The eye is a *loop*
on the end of a line.

DOCKING

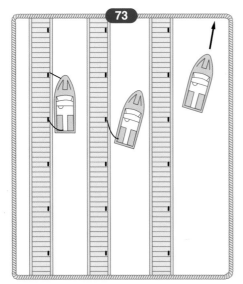

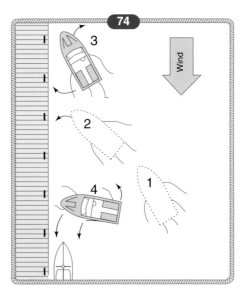

Departing from a Slip (Wind or Current on the Bow): Let go the _____ line and let the wind/current take the bow out or back on a _____ leading spring line to work the bow out, then proceed ahead.

When docking, you're caught in a sudden gust of wind ("**2**" above) from ahead. **What corrective action is required** to avoid getting set-down as shown in position "**4**" above?

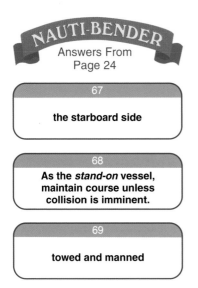

NAUTI-BENDER
Answers From
Page 24

67
the starboard side

68
As the *stand-on* vessel, maintain course unless collision is imminent.

69
towed and manned

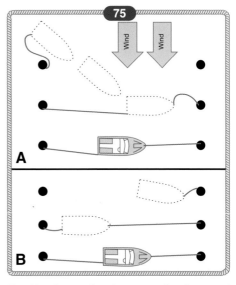

Berthing in restricted space using fore- and aft-mooring buoys or between piles sometimes can be difficult. Which approach, "**A**" or "**B**" shown above would be easier in **strong** cross-wind conditions?

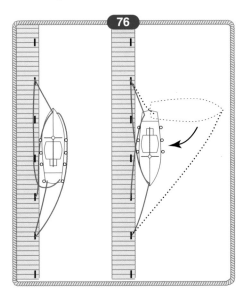

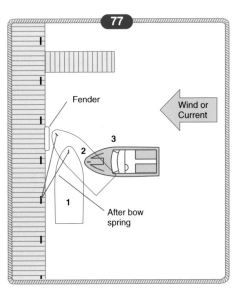

At the dock, turning the boat by hand using lines would most easily be accomplished (as shown above) with the wind or current coming from **ahead** or **astern**?

When departing from a windward berth, use an after bow spring, go **ahead** or **astern** easy with hard **left** or **right** rudder (don't forget fendering).

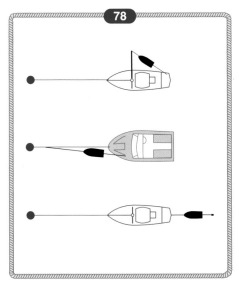

When moored or anchored, a bumping dinghy can be damaging to both the vessel and the crew's sleep. Avoid the bumping by rigging a "_____ _____" to the mooring or boom, or by trailing a _____ off the dinghy's stern.

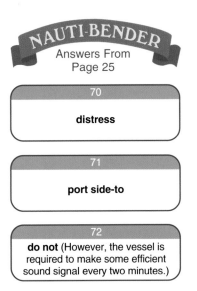

NAUTI-BENDER
Answers From
Page 25

70

distress

71

port side-to

72

do not (However, the vessel is required to make some efficient sound signal every two minutes.)

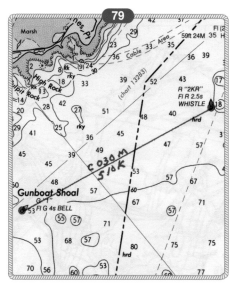

Proceeding from Gunboat Shoal G "1" to R "2KR", a 25-knot wind quickly comes up from 90° relative, affecting your vessel with a 10° "leeway". What course should you now steer?

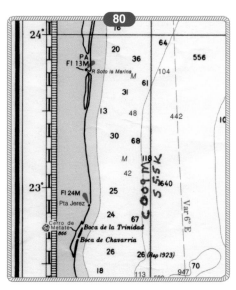

You are under way, cruising at 5.5 knots on course 009M, when Pta Jerez light appears directly off your port beam at 1103. When would you expect to come abeam of R Soto La Marina Light? (Hint: use DR formula 60D = ST.)

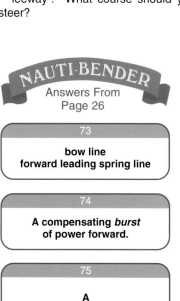

NAUTI-BENDER
Answers From
Page 26

73

bow line
forward leading spring line

74

A compensating *burst*
of power forward.

75

A

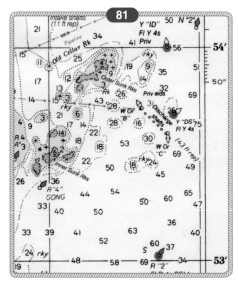

Cruising up the New England coast on your vacation you reach R "2" and set a new course for the next leg to Y "ID". Upon reaching your ETA, the buoy is nowhere in sight... **why**?

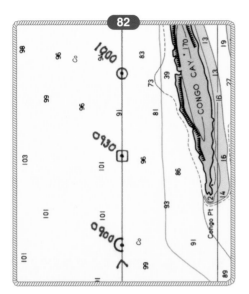

When logging positions on a chart, universal symbols are used: identify the symbols used at (**0900**); (**0930**); and (**1000**) shown above.

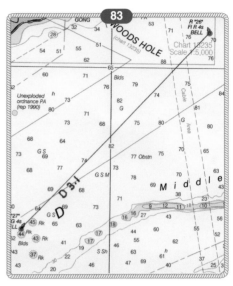

Three nautical miles would be equal to roughly _____ "statute" miles.

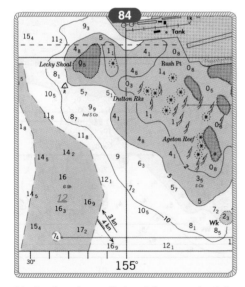

Navigation charts distinguish water depth by color: _____ for deep water; _____ for shallow water; and _____ for land exposed at high tide and submerged at low tide.

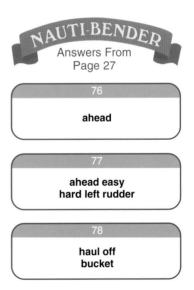

NAUTI-BENDER

Answers From
Page 27

76
ahead

77
ahead easy **hard left rudder**

78
haul off **bucket**

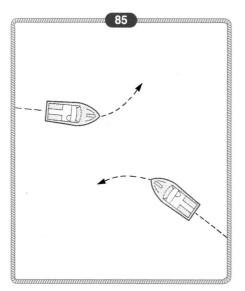

When in doubt between a "crossing" and "head-on" situation, assume a "_____" situation and proceed accordingly.

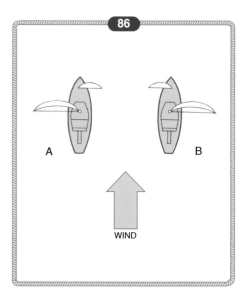

Which of the boats shown above has the right-of-way or is the "stand-on" vessel?

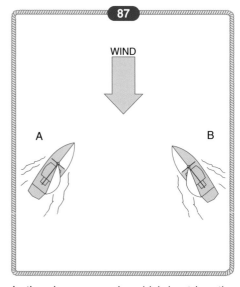

In the above example, which boat has the right-of-way or is the "stand-on" vessel?

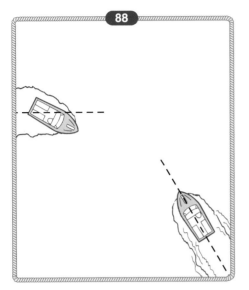

In a head-on, crossing, or overtaking situation, the burdened vessel should make its "_____" known in an obvious and early fashion.

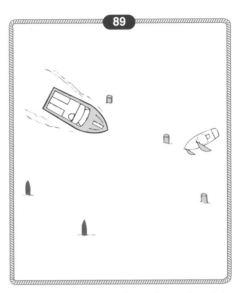

A vessel crossing a river, channel, or fairway must give way to any vessel ascending or descending the water way – **True** or **False**?

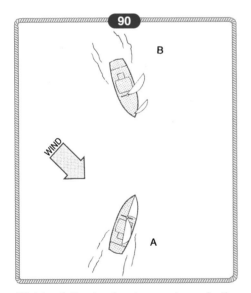

Which of the boats shown above is the "stand-on" vessel or has the right-of-way?

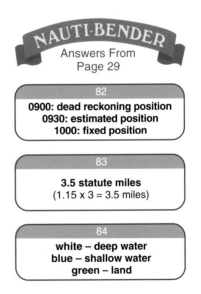

NAUTI-BENDER
Answers From
Page 29

82
0900: dead reckoning position
0930: estimated position
1000: fixed position

83
3.5 statute miles
(1.15 x 3 = 3.5 miles)

84
white – deep water
blue – shallow water
green – land

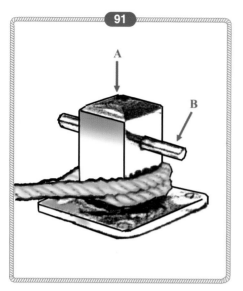

91

(**A**) above is referred to as the " _____ _____ " and (**B**) above is the " _____ _____ ."

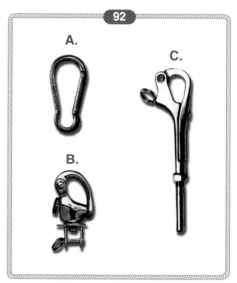

92

A.

C.

B.

Identify the fittings: (**A**) " _____ _____ "; (**B**) " _____ _____ "; and (**C**) " _____ _____ "; shown above.

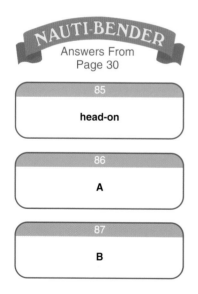

NAUTI-BENDER
Answers From
Page 30

85

head-on

86

A

87

B

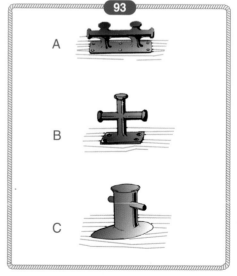

93

A

B

C

Identify the dock fittings: (**A**) " _____ _____ "; (**B**) " _____ _____ "; and (**C**) " _____ " shown above.

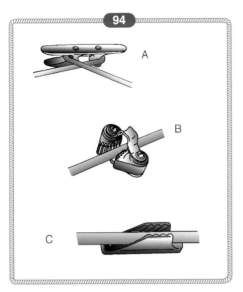

Identify the deck gear shown above.

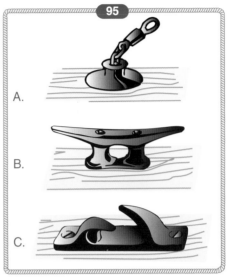

Identify the deck gear shown above: (**A**): "_____ _____", (**B**): "_____", and (**C**): "_____".

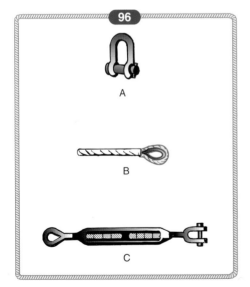

Identify the above.

NAUTI-BENDER
Answers From
Page 31

88
intentions

89
True – must give way

90
B

97

98

Sailing toward an approaching thunderstorm (isolated, not part of a frontal system), the wind will become **stronger** or **weaker**.

Caught in a sudden storm, one option (assuming time availability) would include _____ _____ of the storm to safety.

NAUTI-BENDER
Answers From
Page 32

91
A: Samson post
B: Norman pin

92
A: carabiner hook
B: snap shackle
C: pelican hook

93
A: crosshead bollard
B: staghorn bollard
C: bollard

99

While underway in thick fog, a "man overboard" cry is heard. Not knowing on which side the victim fell, the skipper's next maneuver should be: (A) **stop**; (B) **slow**; or (C) **speed up the engine**.

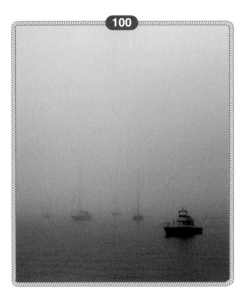

As fog envelops you, you should slow the boat to a speed that will allow you to stop in _____ the distance of your visibility. For example, if your visibility is 200 feet, you should be able to stop in _____ feet.

When Caught in an Approaching Thunderstorm: First, determine your distance from the storm, then decide whether to head for port or ride it out. Thunderstorms can travel up to _____ miles per hour.

In fog, extra care and vigilance should be taken when approaching sea buoys, because numerous vessels could be heading for the _____ navigational aid!

Answers From
Page 33

94
A: jam cleat
B: cam cleat
C: clam cleat

95
A: chain pipe
B: cleat
C: chock

96
A: shackle
B: thimble
C: turnbuckle

103

104

WELCOME ABOARD SAFETY TALK AND MINI-TOUR

1. Location of refuse containers (nothing goes overboard but bait).
2. Location and use of safety gear.
3. How to put life jackets on.
4. Use of the VHF radio (specifically the emergency channel 16 and the squelch control).
5. Proper use of the marine head.
6. Crew-overboard procedures.
7. General on-board basic rules.

PHOTO: COURTESY OF THE U.S. COAST GUARD

PHOTO: COURTESY OF BOSTON WHALER BOATS

The *Flotation Aid* (Type III PFD) is the most comfortable PFD and **will** or **will not** keep the wearer's face (if unconscious) out of the water.

It's a beautiful, sunny day and you're fishing ten miles offshore with some non-boater friends. Unfortunately, while weighing anchor, you fall overboard. What will happen next?

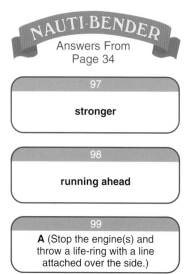

NAUTI-BENDER
Answers From Page 34

97
stronger

98
running ahead

99
A (Stop the engine(s) and throw a life-ring with a line attached over the side.)

105

PHOTO: COURTESY OF THE U.S. COAST GUARD

Marine meteor flares are available in two colors: _____ for non-emergency signaling and _____ for emergency signaling. They have a burn time of _____ to _____ seconds, depending on the type.

106

WHAT TO DO WHEN YOU RUN OUT OF GAS

1. Conserve electrical power.
2. In shallow water drop the anchor immediately.
3. In deep water drop the anchor with about 50' of line for a sea anchor.
4. Check bilges for fumes and fuel.
5. Everyone should don life jackets.
6. Alert nearby boats and ask them to stand by. If they can't assist, radio a towing service for fuel.

PHOTO: COURTESY OF BOSTON WHALER BOATS

Carrying spare fuel in a portable tank will ensure that you probably won't run out of fuel... **True** or **False**?

107

PHOTO: COURTESY OF THE U.S. COAST GUARD

"If we were not late, I'd top off... but we should be fine." "If we cut this buoy we'll save time." "I forgot to ventilate the engine compartment." Boating happens in a potentially _____ environment and doesn't reward the hasty and rushed.

108

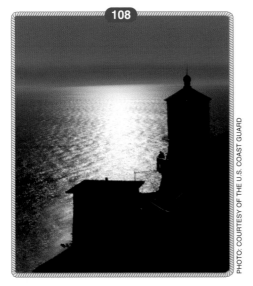

PHOTO: COURTESY OF THE U.S. COAST GUARD

Safety Tip: Most experienced seamen never get underway at night without a _____ or pocket-size strobe light on their person.

NAUTI-BENDER
Answers From
Page 35

100

**half the distance
100 feet**

101

20 miles per hour

102

the same navigational aid

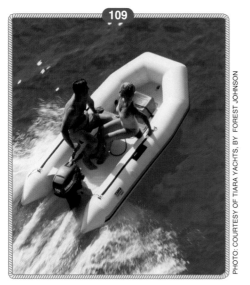

A fully inflated RIB rides better and lasts longer. It is properly inflated when: (A) **you can't pump any more**; (B) **the back pressure lifts your foot off the pump**; or (C) **the side wall "feels right" to the touch**.

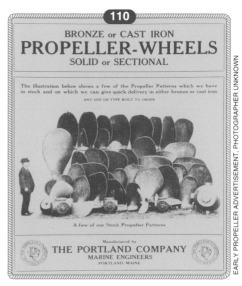

Theoretically, how far will a 15¾" X 17" propeller push the boat forward (in inches) with each revolution of the prop?

NAUTI-BENDER
Answers From
Page 36

103
will not
(Not recommended for
blue water boating.)

104
Before leaving, you always give
a short safety talk to all non-
crew guests... **you're rescued!**

105
white: non-emergency
red: emergency
6 to 40 seconds

A ship's clock strikes on the half-hour in four-hour cycles: first half-hour – one bell; first hour – two bells; first hour and a half – three bells, etc. The end of the cycle is indicated by _____ bells.

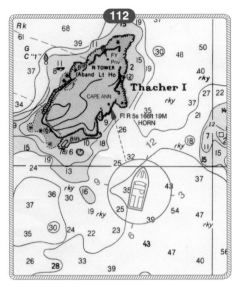

A lookout should report sighted objects using: (A) **true bearings**; (B) **magnetic bearings**; (C) **relative bearings**; or (D) **the clock notation system**.

Spinnaker sheets should be _____ the length of the boat and the genoa sheets should be _____ and _____ its length.

Binoculars are rated by magnification and the **diameter**, **length**, or **thickness** of the lens (millimeters). A 7X50 binocular, excellent for on-the-water use, has a magnification of _____ times and a _____ millimeter diameter lens.

NAUTI-BENDER
Answers From
Page 37

106

True – However, the fire hazard is far greater than the danger of running out of fuel.

107

potentially hostile environment

108

flashlight

To avoid kinks while coiling **three-stranded** or **braided** line, twist your wrist a quarter turn **clockwise** or **counterclockwise** with each loop.

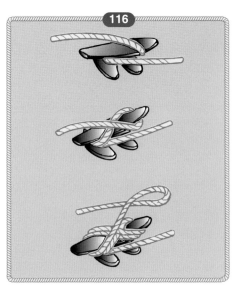

Typically, lines are properly fastened to dock cleats by a "_____ turn", two figure eights, and concluded with a half-hitch.

NAUTI-BENDER
Answers From Page 38

109

B: When the back pressure lifts your foot off the pump.

110

17 inches

111

eight bells at noon, 4 PM, 8 PM, midnight, 4 AM, and 8 AM

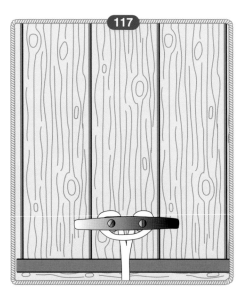

The above depicts the proper method to secure an eye to an onboard cleat that will hold well under **strain** or **no strain**.

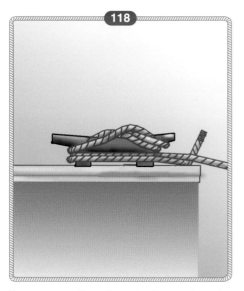

Prevent your lines from chafing on the edge of the dock (ebbing tide) by wrapping several turns of the excess (after cleating) _____ the standing part.

PHOTO: COURTESY OF THE U.S. COAST GUARD

A most effective method for "_____" a line with a monkey fist is illustrated above. Hint: throw a regular dock line underhand as you would a bowling ball and aim to the side of the catcher.

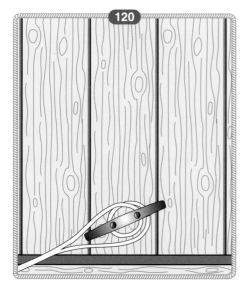

The above *belaying* technique is useful for single handed _____-_____ line handling. When ready, the slack line can be flipped off of the cleat.

NAUTI-BENDER

Answers From
Page 39

112

C or D

113

**twice
one and one-half**

114

**diameter of the lens
seven times
fifty millimeter lens**

PHOTO: COURTESY OF AQUASPORT BOATS

After a long day of "gunkholing", you notice an increased amount of vibration in the boat. How can you check whether the problem is in the engine or in the drive train/propeller?

Winter Layup – Final Step: Wrap the exhaust port/prop with plastic and duct tape to keep out **dirt and debris**; **snow and ice buildup**; or **small furry critters**.

NAUTI-BENDER
Answers From
Page 40

115

three-stranded line (No twist necessary with braided line.)
clockwise

116

round turn

117

no strain

PHOTO: COURTESY OF BERTRAM YACHTS

After winter layup, your boat's head is not working. You determine that the discharge line is clogged with waste. Your best approach would be to flush the line with a mild solution of: **sulphuric acid**; **muriatic acid**; or **lye/vinegar**.

PHOTO: COURTESY OF BOSTON WHALER BOATS

Add Life to Your Trailer Tires (during long-term storage): Block up the trailer to take the weight off the tires; **increase** or **lower** the air pressure; and cover the tires to protect them from the sun's UV rays.

"Old Salts" Remedy: If your plastic port-holes have minor scratches... try polishing with smooth _____ butter to bring back the original clarity... keep the remainder onboard in case you get shipwrecked.

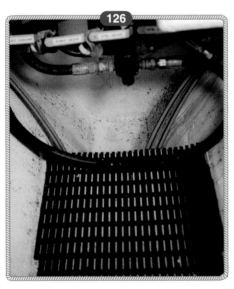

A mildew colony can be killed by washing the gelcoat surface with chlorine bleach that is mixed with an equal volume of water. To discourage regrowth, wipe the surface with _____ _____ _____.

NAUTI-BENDER
Answers From
Page 41

118
under the standing part

119
heaving a line

120
eye-ashore **line handling**

Wind as a Weather Clue: Winds from the north, northwest, and southwest typically bring _____ weather. Winds from the south, east, and northeast deliver _____ weather.

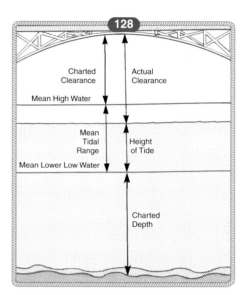

Charted Clearance
Actual Clearance
Mean High Water
Mean Tidal Range
Height of Tide
Mean Lower Low Water
Charted Depth

Since chart depths are typically given as Mean Lower Low Water, the actual water depth will generally be **higher** or **lower** than that shown on the chart.

NAUTI-BENDER
Answers From
Page 42

121
Rev the engine in neutral. If there is no vibration, the problem is in the drive train.

122
small furry critters
(They love to make their winter residence in the exhaust port.)

123
muriatic acid

Tidal currents run **stronger** or **weaker** over shallows, alongshore, in open ocean, and along straight coasts.

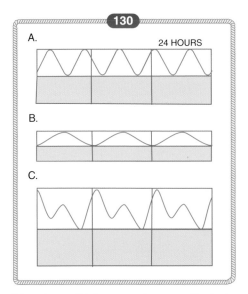

The above tidal range diagrams illustrate: "**A**": semi-diurnal tides; "**B**": diurnal tides; and "**C**": "_____" tides.

Wind direction can be most accurately estimated by observing the: **swells**; **waves**; **cloud movement**; or **none of the above**.

Determine the Wind's Speed by Observation: For example, a fresh breeze (force 5) with winds between _____ and _____ mph would be accompanied by some white caps, waves between 1.5' and 2.5' and flags rippling.

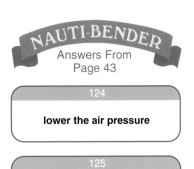

NAUTI-BENDER
Answers From
Page 43

124

lower the air pressure

125

smooth peanut butter

126

apple cider vinegar

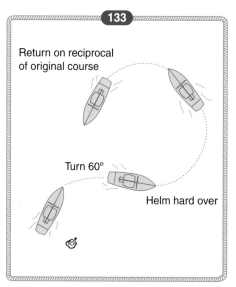

133

Return on reciprocal of original course

Turn 60°

Helm hard over

Williamson Turn execution: Put your helm hard over until reaching the original course 025° plus 60° (i.e. 085°), then put the helm hard over (opposite direction) until reaching the _____ of the original course or _____°.

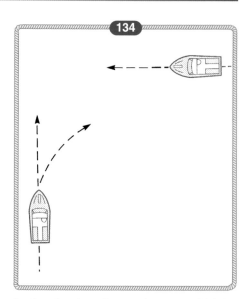

134

In the situation shown above, would it be better practice to **speed up and cross ahead of** or **slow down and pass aft** of the other vessel?

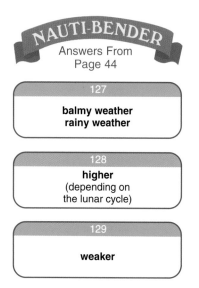

NAUTI-BENDER
Answers From
Page 44

127
balmy weather
rainy weather

128
higher
(depending on the lunar cycle)

129
weaker

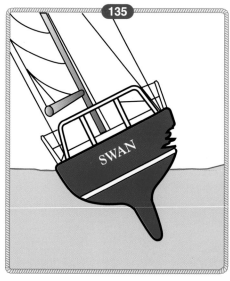

135

SWAN

Situation: You've hit a submerged log, holed the boat and are leaking badly. To make matters worse, the hole is not accessible from the inside. **What other steps can be taken to stop or decrease the leak**?

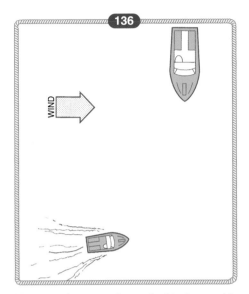

You are about to take a disabled vessel in tow. She appears to have more leeway than your vessel. To pass the tow rope, you should approach from: (A) **off your port bow**; (B) **off your starboard bow**; or (C) **from head-on**.

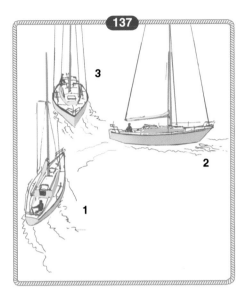

As illustrated above, it will be easier to execute a tight turn **up**- or **down**-**wind**: going ahead ("**2**" above) the wind will blow the bow around; and then in "**3**" above, while in reverse, the "_____ - _____" will kick the stern around.

When grounded, protect the boat from being badly _____ and possibly _____ by placing fenders, cushions, etc. between the hull and the sea bed.

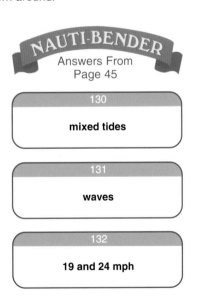

NAUTI-BENDER
Answers From
Page 45

130
mixed tides

131
waves

132
19 and 24 mph

While docked, a boat is prevented from sawing back and forth by its "_____ lines".

Locking Technique: For more control and easy departure, "_____" bow and stern lines should be utilized and these lines should always be tended, not cleated (especially on the way down).

Answers From
Page 46

133

**reciprocal
205°**

134

**slow down and pass aft
of the other vessel**
(Less chance of collision.)

135

**Patch the hole from the outside
or run to safety heeled over or
up on plane.**

When entering a lock, be prepared for any mooring situation by having _____ and _____ rigged on both sides of the vessel.

When passing through a lock, which is the best side to moor to?

Locking Strategy: When picking a spot to moor within a lock, try to avoid the gate ends where the _____ and _____ will be the strongest.

Why is it usually a good practice for a smaller boat to enter a lock last?

NAUTI-BENDER
Answers From
Page 47

136
off your starboard bow (Less chance of the disabled vessel being "set-down" on your boat.)

137
**up-wind
prop-effect**

138
**damaged
holed**

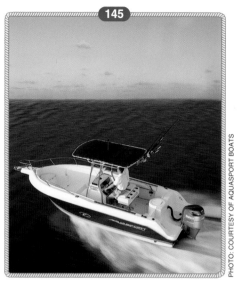

Yards-Per-Minute Rule: "In one minute a vessel making three knots will cover 100 yards". What distance (miles) will a vessel making 15 knots travel in four minutes?

PHOTO: COURTESY OF AQUASPORT BOATS

A wind vane on a moving vessel indicates the **true** or **apparent** wind direction.

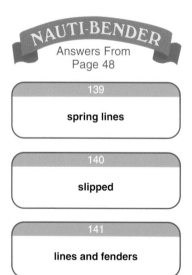

NAUTI-BENDER
Answers From
Page 48

139
spring lines

140
slipped

141
lines and fenders

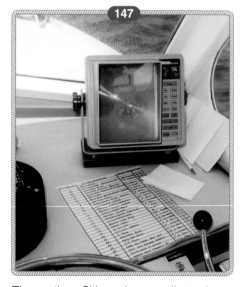

The cautious Skipper has excellent primary electronics (GPS, Loran, VHF, etc.), battery-powered backup instruments, plus he/she will maintain hard copy backups: charts; _____ lists; etc.

To easily find your way back to an unfamiliar harbor, channel, etc... look _____ when departing and take mental images of the harbor entrance, buoys, landmarks, etc.

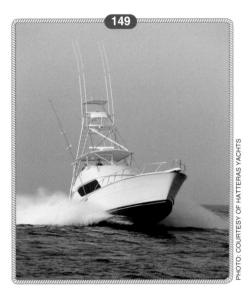

PHOTO: COURTESY OF HATTERAS YACHTS

To convert knots into miles-per-hour, multiply knots by _____ .

You are entering an unfamiliar harbor. To see more detail on the chart plotter, the scale should be changed from: (A) **1:3,300,000** to **1:33,000,000**; (B) **1:300** to **1:3,000**; or (C) **1:3,000** to **1:300**.

NAUTI-BENDER
Answers From
Page 49

142
The windward side.
(Where the wind will
hold off the vessel.)

143
currents and eddies

144
This enables rafting along-side
larger vessels... thus
minimizing line handling.

In rough anchorages fiberglass "_____" are just what the Cap'n ordered to avoid wear and tear on the side of your boat and the dock.

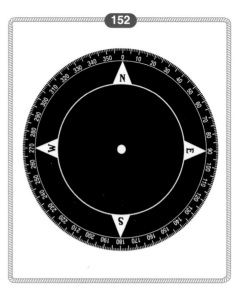

The four principal compass points: north, south, east, and west are commonly referr-ed to as the "_____ _____".

NAUTI-BENDER
Answers From
Page 50

145

1 nautical mile
(4 x 100 x 5 = 2000 yds)

146

apparent wind

147

waypoint lists

When a waterskier says he/she is skiing "22 off"... how long is his/her ski rope?

PHOTO: COURTESY OF THE U.S. COAST GUARD

"_____" is the error in compass readings (usually different amounts east, west and so on) caused by onboard ferrous materials or electronic equipment.

The "lee" is the side **toward or away from** which the wind blows... an object sheltered from the wind is "in the lee".

An amateur yachtsman is sometimes referred to as a "_____".

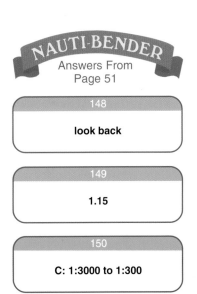

The approximate distance to a storm's center can be determined by noting a barometer's hourly rate of fall. Assuming a 0.08 to 0.12 inch/hour fall, what is the approximate distance to the storm's center?

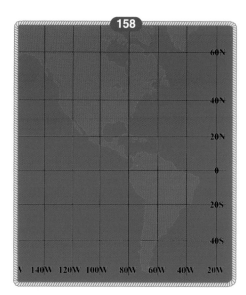

In the United States, weather typically moves from **east to west** or from **west to east**. Cold fronts move about 500 statute miles-per-day, while warm fronts move about 200 miles-per-day.

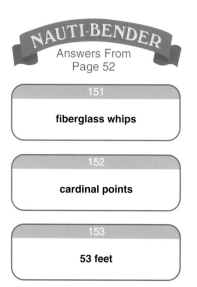

NAUTI-BENDER
Answers From
Page 52

151
fiberglass whips

152
cardinal points

153
53 feet

"Sun Dog": A halo around the sun or moon will accurately forecast rain about _____ percent (sun) and _____ percent (moon) of the times viewed.

Typically, current runs **faster** or **slower** in deep water and **faster** or **slower** in shallow water.

Ocean experts estimate that a one-knot current running against wind-driven waves will: **double**; **triple**; or **quadruple** the waves' size.

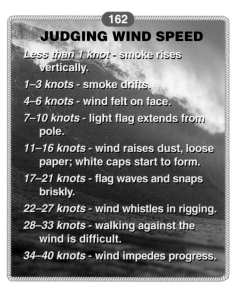

JUDGING WIND SPEED

Less than 1 knot - smoke rises vertically.

1–3 knots - smoke drifts.

4–6 knots - wind felt on face.

7–10 knots - light flag extends from pole.

11–16 knots - wind raises dust, loose paper; white caps start to form.

17–21 knots - flag waves and snaps briskly.

22–27 knots - wind whistles in rigging.

28–33 knots - walking against the wind is difficult.

34–40 knots - wind impedes progress.

Which of the above is incorrect?

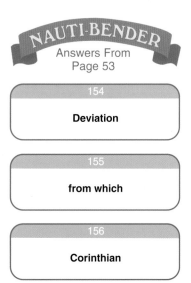

NAUTI-BENDER

Answers From
Page 53

154
Deviation

155
from which

156
Corinthian

163

You're on a collision course with a boat pulling a waterskier off your port bow. Who has the right-of-way?

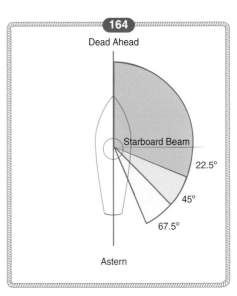

164

Dead Ahead

Starboard Beam

22.5°

45°

67.5°

Astern

How many degrees abaft the beam of the vessel ahead must a boat be to be considered "overtaking": **22.5°**; **45°**; or **67°**?

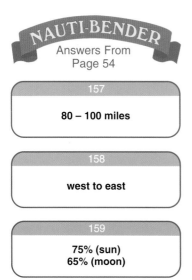

NAUTI-BENDER
Answers From
Page 54

157

80 – 100 miles

158

west to east

159

75% (sun)
65% (moon)

165

Sailing down an inland river you note that you are on a rapidly closing collision course with a tug pushing a barge (down-stream)... who has the right-of-way or is the "stand-on vessel"?

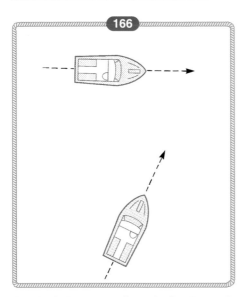

If in doubt between a "crossing" or "overtaking" situation, assume _____ and proceed accordingly.

You're the only person who is ever aboard your 16' fishing boat. To pass a C.G. Courtesy Marine Examination your boat would be required to have: (A) **one wearable**; (B) **two wearable**; or (C) **two wearable and one throwable Type IV PFDs**.

PHOTO: COURTESY OF U.S. COAST GUARD

How much oil or fuel discharged overboard is considered by the Coast Guard as "reportable or "chargeable"? What is the maximum civil penalty for discharging oil in U.S waters?

Answers From
Page 55

160
faster (deep water)
slower (shallow water)

161
double the waves' size

162
11–16 knots (White caps begin to form between 7–10 knots or 8–12 mph.)

169

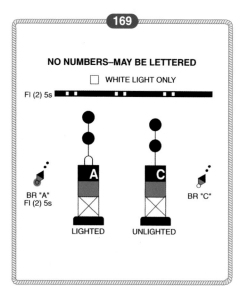

NO NUMBERS—MAY BE LETTERED

☐ WHITE LIGHT ONLY

Fl (2) 5s

A

C

BR "A"
Fl (2) 5s

BR "C"

LIGHTED   UNLIGHTED

Buoys with red and black bands indicate an
_____ _____.

170

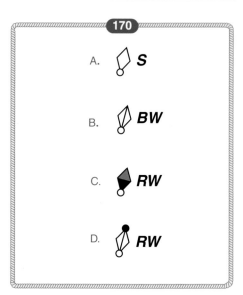

A.   S

B.   BW

C.   RW

D.   RW

Which of the chart buoy symbols shown
above indicates a safe-water mark?

171

Proceeding upstream on a river using the
"Uniform State Buoyage System" you
encounter a buoy with alternating red and
white stripes, indicating that you should
pass between the buoy and the nearest or
farthest shore.

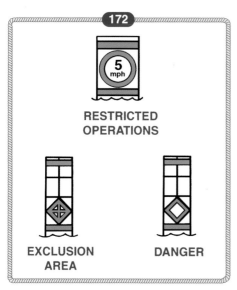

172

5 mph

RESTRICTED OPERATIONS

EXCLUSION AREA

DANGER

"_____ _____ _____ buoys are white with orange stripes.

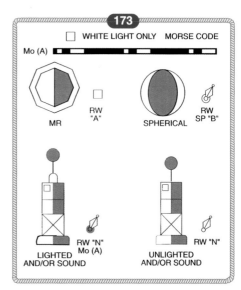

173

☐ WHITE LIGHT ONLY   MORSE CODE

Mo (A) ▮▮▮▮▮▮▮▮▮▮

MR

RW "A"

SPHERICAL

RW SP "B"

LIGHTED AND/OR SOUND

RW "N" Mo (A)

UNLIGHTED AND/OR SOUND

RW "N"

As defined by the U.S. Aids to Navigation System, spherical buoys may be: **numbered**; **lettered**; **lighted**; **sounded**; or **all of the above**.

174

When "running" **upstream** or **downstream** in waters using the "Uniform State Buoyage System", a boat should pass between black buoys to port and red buoys to starboard.

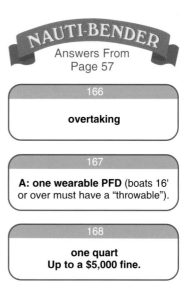

NAUTI-BENDER
Answers From
Page 57

166

overtaking

167

A: one wearable PFD (boats 16' or over must have a "throwable").

168

one quart
Up to a $5,000 fine.

A braided towline is preferable to three-strand nylon because the same diameter braided line is stronger; does not kink; and is elastic but not too elastic to create a _____-_____ hazard.

When towing alongside, the towboat's stern should be: **even with**; **aft of**; or **forward of** the other boat's transom for better control.

NAUTI-BENDER
Answers From
Page 58

169
an isolated danger
(normally anchored
above the danger)

170
D

171
farthest shore

The maximum speed that a "displacement boat" can make is governed by her _____ _____ and can be determined by what formula?

178

PHOTO: COURTESY OF BOSTON WHALER BOATS, BY MIKE FULLER

Trailer Loading Procedure: Back in, until the bunks are completely submerged... **why**? Then, pull forward until the tops of the trailer's fenders are barely awash. Finally, "power load" or float the boat onto the trailer.

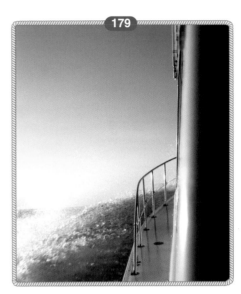

179

Which of the following sea conditions would offer the most comfortable ride in heavy weather: **a head sea from broad on the bow**; **a beam sea**; **a quartering sea**; or **a following sea**?

180

PHOTO: COURTESY OF ALDEN YACHTS

You're running a twin-screw boat going ahead with rudders amidships. If the port engine suddenly stops, the boat will: **go to port**; **go to starboard**; **continue on a straight course**.

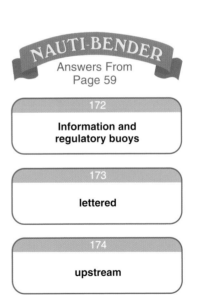

NAUTI-BENDER
Answers From
Page 59

172

Information and regulatory buoys

173

lettered

174

upstream

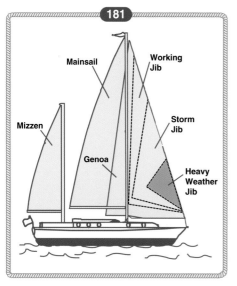

181

In the above diagram, which two sail descriptors have been transposed?

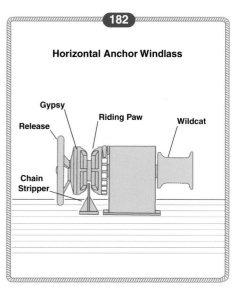

182

Horizontal Anchor Windlass

In the above diagram, which two descriptors have been transposed?

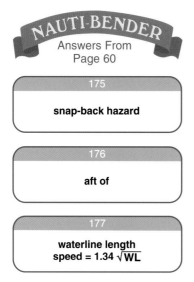

NAUTI-BENDER

Answers From
Page 60

175

snap-back hazard

176

aft of

177

waterline length
speed = $1.34 \sqrt{WL}$

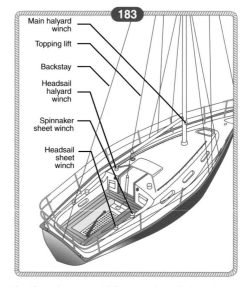

183

Main halyard winch
Topping lift
Backstay
Headsail halyard winch
Spinnaker sheet winch
Headsail sheet winch

In the above, which two descriptors have been transposed?

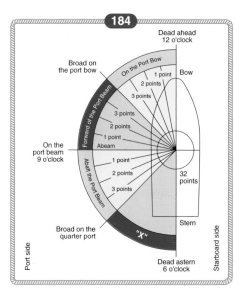

Language Under Way: An object bearing at point "**X**" (shown above) would be referred to as "_____ _____ _____ _____ _____ _____."

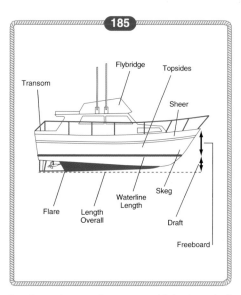

In the above diagram, which two hull descriptors have been transposed?

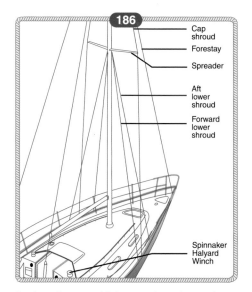

In the above, which two descriptors have been transposed?

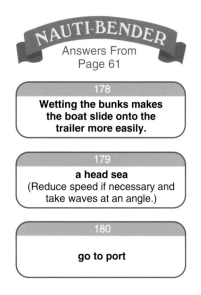

NAUTI-BENDER
Answers From
Page 61

178

Wetting the bunks makes the boat slide onto the trailer more easily.

179

a head sea
(Reduce speed if necessary and take waves at an angle.)

180

go to port

PHOTO: COURTESY OF SEATOW

The Essence of Good Seamanship: staying out of _____ and getting out of _____ if you should get into it.

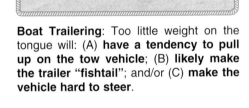

Boat Trailering: Too little weight on the tongue will: (A) **have a tendency to pull up on the tow vehicle**; (B) **likely make the trailer "fishtail"**; and/or (C) **make the vehicle hard to steer**.

Answers From
Page 62

181
"Heavy Weather Jib" should be "Storm Jib" and vice versa.

182
"Gypsy" has been transposed with "Wildcat" and vice versa.

183
"Spinnaker sheet winch" has been transposed with "headsail sheet winch" and vice versa.

PHOTO: COURTESY OF TIARA YACHTS

What does the master navigator give his sweetheart for Valentine's Day?

Boat Trailering: Too much weight on the tongue will: (A) **put undue strain on the tow vehicle's suspension**; (B) **make the vehicle hard to steer**; (C) **likely make the trailer "fishtail"**; or (D) **all of the above**.

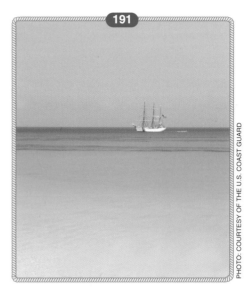

PHOTO: COURTESY OF THE U.S. COAST GUARD

Nautical Trivia: Ocean water is the most blue where there is the **least** or **most** abundance of sea life.

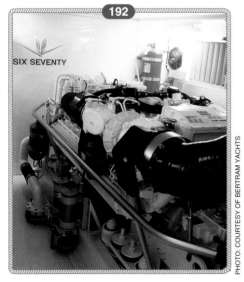

PHOTO: COURTESY OF BERTRAM YACHTS

To determine the torque your engine is producing at any one point in time, you need to know the engine's: (A) **rpms**; (B) **horsepower**; (C) **compression ratio**; and/or (D) **bore & stroke**.

Answers From Page 63

184

two points on the port quarter

185

"Flare" should be "Skeg" and vice versa.

186

"Forward lower shroud" should be "Aft lower shroud" and vice versa.

Aromatherapy: After a long winter lay up, you note that the boat smells worse than a high school gym locker. Try placing a few drops of **wintergreen oil**, **penetrol**, or **mink oil** on cotton balls (in a glass) and place in strategic locations.

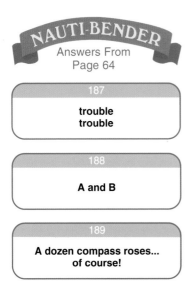

NAUTI-BENDER
Answers From
Page 64

187

trouble
trouble

188

A and B

189

A dozen compass roses...
of course!

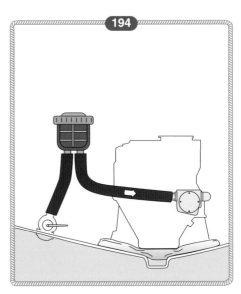

To avoid pumping oil or other contaminants overboard via the bilge pump, you may want to consider placing a bilge "_____" under your engine(s).

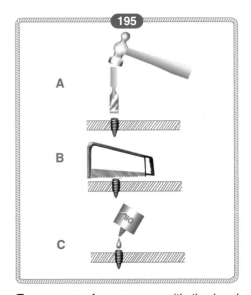

To remove a frozen screw with the head sheared off: (A) **bang smartly with a hammer**; (B) **cut (hacksaw) or chisel a slot in the remaining shank**; (C) **treat with "Liquid Wrench"**; or (D) **all of the above**.

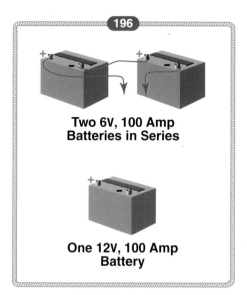

Two 6V, 100 Amp Batteries in Series

One 12V, 100 Amp Battery

Which battery configuration shown above will provide more cranking power?

Varmints Verboten: Inside boat storage creates a great winter condo for small furry creatures with long tails. To thwart these non-invited guests place mothballs or a few drops of _____ oil in storage areas.

To control the amount of paint on your brush, stretch a wide rubber band around the can vertically and wipe the brush against it. What other advantage is gained by using this procedure?

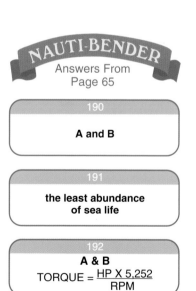

NAUTI-BENDER
Answers From
Page 65

190
A and B

191
the least abundance of sea life

192
A & B

$$\text{TORQUE} = \frac{\text{HP X 5,252}}{\text{RPM}}$$

Red lights displayed under a single-span bridge indicate: (A) **that you should stop**; (B) **the channel's boundaries**; or (C) **danger ahead, proceed with caution**.

"_____ group flashing lights" have different groups of flashes at regular intervals.

NAUTI-BENDER
Answers From Page 66

193
wintergreen oil (The boat will smell minty fresh for months.)

194
pillow (an oil-absorbing sponge)

195
D: all of the above

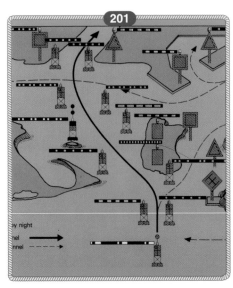

Entering an unfamiliar harbor at night, you notice several lighted buoys flashing at different intervals. If you are looking for a "Morse" buoy, it will be a **white** or **green/red** light cycling a _____ and _____ flash.

202

"_____ _____ _____ **flashing**" lights have a fixed light interrupted regularly by groups of two or more flashing lights (usually a different color).

203

PHOTO: COURTESY OF BERTRAM YACHTS

Cruising at night, you observe a vessel with a flashing amber light (three-second intervals) indicating the presence of a _____.

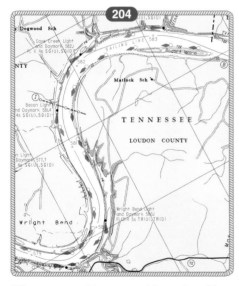

204

When a vessel is approaching a bend in a river where oncoming traffic cannot be seen, should the vessel sound one or two prolonged blast(s)?

NAUTI-BENDER
Answers From
Page 67

196

**two 6V, 100 Amp
batteries in series**

197

spearmint oil
(It can be purchased at your local pharmacy.)

198

The paint drips right back into the can – not onto the rim or down the sides.

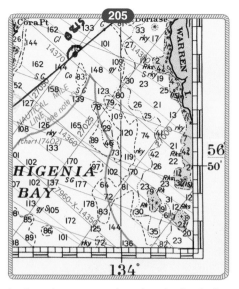

In the above example, what is the lat/lon position at 0815?

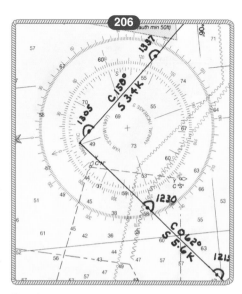

Dead reckoning or "DR" positions are determined by calculating the vessel's position using courses steered and distances made. The term "dead" evolved from "ded", the abbreviated form of _____.

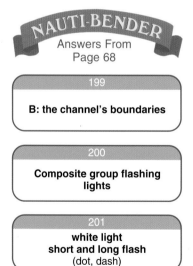

NAUTI-BENDER
Answers From Page 68

199

B: the channel's boundaries

200

Composite group flashing lights

201

white light
short and long flash
(dot, dash)

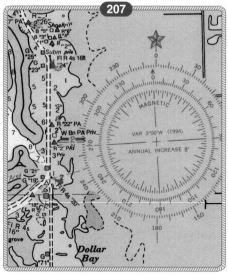

What true and magnetic course would you follow from light "20" to light "24"?

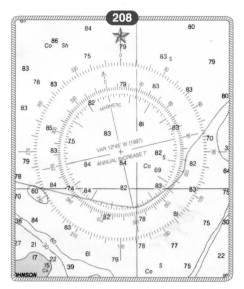

Most recreational boaters can navigate very accurately by using the inner ring (magnetic) on a chart's compass rose, and need not worry about converting to true courses – **True** or **False**.

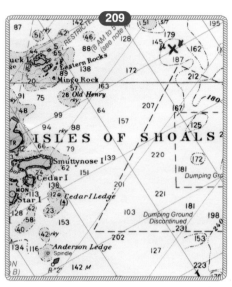

You are cod fishing at R "2" when you hear a Mayday call on channel 16. The boat (point "**X**" above) is about 9 miles away. Your vessel's top speed is 15 knots... **how long will it take you to reach the victims**?

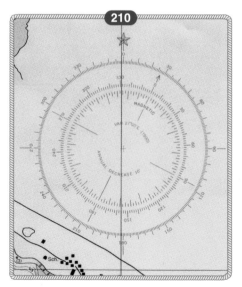

Cruising in an area where the variation is east, the *compass* course will usually be **more** or **less** than the *true* course.

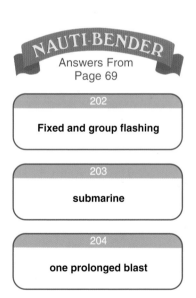

NAUTI-BENDER

Answers From
Page 69

202
Fixed and group flashing

203
submarine

204
one prolonged blast

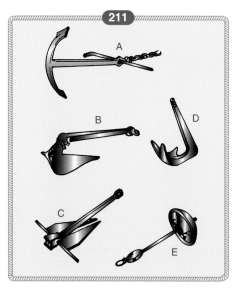

211

Identify the numbers of the following anchor types with the letters shown above: **1.** Mushroom; **2.** Danforth; **3.** Plough; **4.** Fisherman; and **5.** Bruce. Which anchor is typically **not** used by recreational boaters?

212

"_____ _____": A deck fitting used on larger vessels to temporarily prevent the anchor chain from running out, thereby taking the strain off the windlass.

NAUTI-BENDER
Answers From
Page 70

205
56° 54' N **134° 03' W**

206
deduced

207
000T **003M**

213

"_____ the luff" is a quick and simple method of temporarily "jamming" or stopping all movement of a line through a block.

A "_____" vent allows air to enter below decks while blocking incoming spray. In rough weather the "cowl" should be turned **forward** or **aft**?

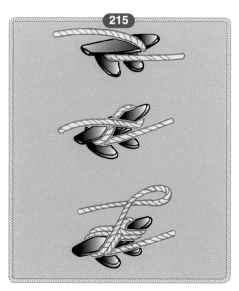

Typically, lines are properly fastened to dock cleats by a "_____ turn", two figure eights, and concluded with a half-hitch.

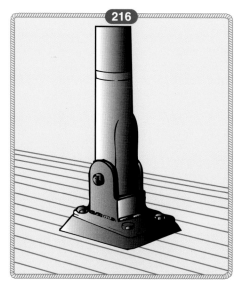

"_____": a fitting, typically made of metal, fixed to a sailing vessel's deck in which the "foot" of a lowered mast is "stepped".

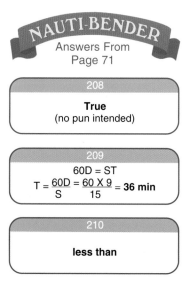

NAUTI-BENDER
Answers From
Page 71

208

True
(no pun intended)

209

$$60D = ST$$
$$T = \frac{60D}{S} = \frac{60 \times 9}{15} = \textbf{36 min}$$

210

less than

The best tide conditions for crossing a rough bar would be _____ _____, _____ water.

To estimate your visibility in fog, drop a small ball of paper overboard and note the time it takes to _____. The navigator can then work out the distance.

NAUTI-BENDER
Answers From Page 72

211
1: E; 2: C; 3: B; 4: A; 5: D
The Mushroom (E) is typically used for moorings.

212
Devil's claw

213
Choking the luff

***Heaving to* in a Powerboat**: Steer into the wind at a heading that takes the waves on either side of the bow while adjusting the throttle(s) to provide steerage but minimal _____.

220

What is the first action a Skipper should take if he/she senses fog is beginning to form?

221

PHOTO: COURTESY OF THE U.S. COAST GUARD

If executed properly, running an inlet (high, following sea) on the back of a wave is quite effective. However, running too far _____ may result in broaching or pitchpoling; running too far _____ may result in being "pooped".

222

PHOTO: COURTESY OF THE U.S. COAST GUARD

Lying Ahull: The boat's tiller is lashed to **leeward** or **windward** and the boat runs under *bare poles* at a right angle to the wind (taking seas on the beam).

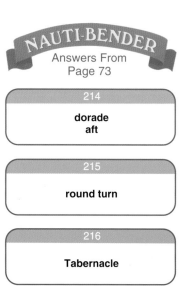

NAUTI-BENDER
Answers From Page 73

214

dorade
aft

215

round turn

216

Tabernacle

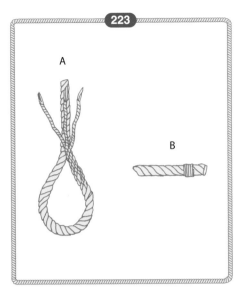

"**A**" above: When making an eye splice on the end of a line, how many "tucks" are recommended? "**B**" above: The "lay" of a line refers to the _____ of the twist in the strands.

The "_____-_____" knot is used as a stopper to prevent a line from running through a block or a grommet.

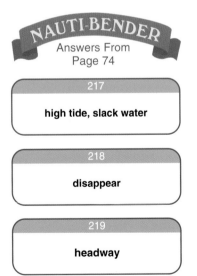

A way of fastening two lines of the same diameter is to use a _____ bend.

226

The "_____" or "square knot" is not recommended to lengthen lines and should be used sparingly.

227

A bowline knot is sometimes used to form a temporary _____ at the end of a line.

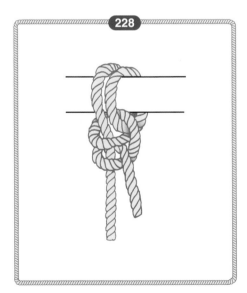

228

The "_____ knot", or fisherman's bend, is used to secure a line to a buoy or to the ring of an anchor.

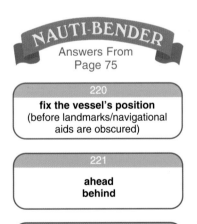

NAUTI-BENDER
Answers From
Page 75

220

fix the vessel's position
(before landmarks/navigational aids are obscured)

221

ahead
behind

222

lashed to leeward (Caution: this tactic should be utilized in winds of 40 knots or less.)

PHOTO: COURTESY OF THE U.S. COAST GUARD

At night, a dim light on the horizon will be seen more quickly by looking: (A) **a little below**; (B) **a little above**; (C) **well below**; or (D) **right at the horizon**.

DAC21665B-97

The last two characters of a boat's **H**ull **I**dentification **N**umber (HIN) indicate **the year the boat was built** or **the model year of the boat.**

NAUTI-BENDER
Answers From
Page 76

223
A: a minimum of five tucks
B: direction of the twist

224
figure-eight knot

225
carrick bend

A yacht broker, when push comes to shove, represents the _____. A marine surveyor represents the person who hires him/her. When in doubt about the condition of a boat... always rely on the **seller**, **surveyor**, or the **yacht broker**.

PHOTO: COURTESY OF GRADY WHITE BOATS

Engine/steering controls on smaller boats are typically installed on the boat's starboard side... to provide the Skipper with better visibility of his/her "_____ _____".

There is a new launch driver at your yacht club. You are happy to see that he is dropping off and picking up passengers on the proper side of the boats... which is?

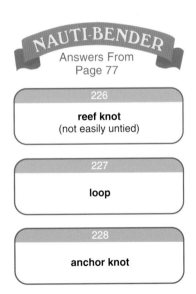

NAUTI-BENDER
Answers From
Page 77

226
reef knot
(not easily untied)

227
loop

228
anchor knot

Rule-of-Thumb: To ensure that your "tender" will achieve a maximum speed of 25 knots, divide the boat's weight (loaded) by _____ to determine the engine's required horse power.

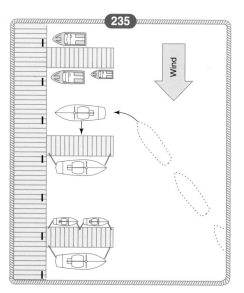

Docking Into a Windward Slip: Put her into neutral and coast in; apply short "bursts" astern or rig a _____ line to stop the boat's forward motion; and let the wind move you gently alongside.

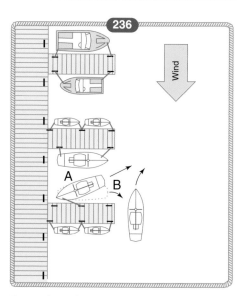

Departing a Windward Berth: Either spring off the **bow** or **stern**, or "walk" the boat to the end of the pier and motor off into the wind.

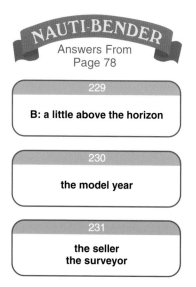

NAUTI-BENDER
Answers From
Page 78

229
B: a little above the horizon

230
the model year

231
the seller   **the surveyor**

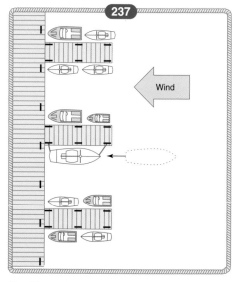

Docking Head Into the Wind (assuming good reverse control): Motor into the slip; use a forward burst to stop the boat's momentum; and secure the _____ line first.

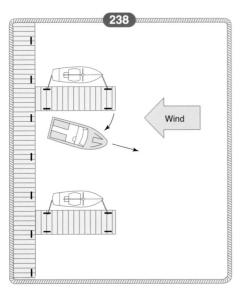

Departing Head Into the Wind: _____ the bow off and motor straight out.

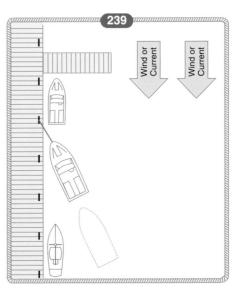

Docking Into a Strong Wind or Tidal Current: Approach the pier at the tightest possible angle; secure the bow line; and let the boat _____ back into position.

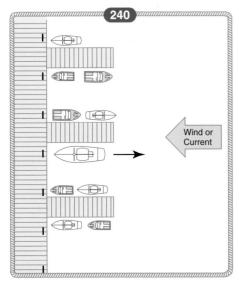

Departing Stern Into the Wind (with a single-screw boat): Back out ... the boat will back to _____ and clear the pier nicely; or if poor reverse control, "walk the boat" out to the end of the pier and motor off.

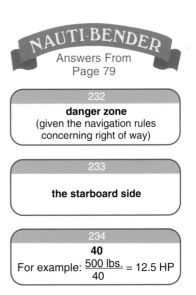

NAUTI-BENDER
Answers From
Page 79

232
danger zone
(given the navigation rules concerning right of way)

233
the starboard side

234
40
For example: $\frac{500 \text{ lbs.}}{40} = 12.5$ HP

Spring Commissioning: It's time to put a coat of wax on your Queen Mary. Which of the following should not be waxed, the: **stern drive**; **rubber rubrail**; **non-skid fiberglass surfaces**; or **all of the above**?

When washing down a boat, one can remove black streaks and other stains almost effortlessly by using: (A) **scouring powder**; (B) **boat cleaners with "chelating" agents**; or (C) **a diluted bleach solution**?

Polishing fiberglass boats, especially non-skid areas, is much easier if a _____ _____ rag is utilized.

Cardinal Rules for Cleaning the Boat: Wash often and wash _____ rather than _____; use "boat soap" rather than dish-washing liquid which might remove any wax or polish that you've applied.

When polishing and waxing nooks and crannies around the boat (especially hand rails), a _____ is a highly effective cleaning tool.

PHOTO COURTESY OF ALDEN YACHTS

To extend the shine for up to **30**, **40**, or **50**% longer on newly-cleaned chrome, aluminum, brass, or bronze, apply and buff off a coat of automobile paste wax.

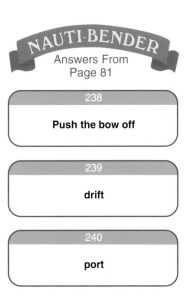

NAUTI-BENDER
Answers From
Page 81

238

Push the bow off

239

drift

240

port

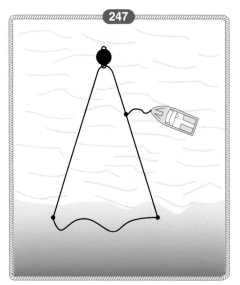

A "_____ - _____" can be rigged for small to relatively large boats and is great in rough anchorages or where there is limited dockage. (Hint: keep the lines well spread apart to avoid tangles.)

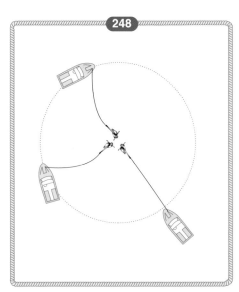

If the Anchor Will Not Break Loose: Power ahead over the anchor and beyond; if that isn't successful, run in a circle while maintaining a _____ until it breaks free.

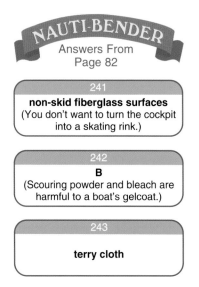

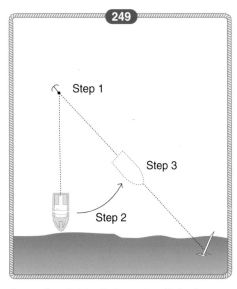

Assuming light winds and sufficient room, the above anchoring technique is simply executed and especially useful in a **flood** or **ebb** tide situation.

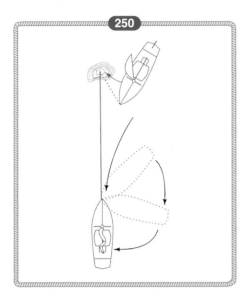

To anchor under sail in **light** or **heavy** air, drop the hook on a run to dig it in quickly without losing steerageway, and proceed as shown above.

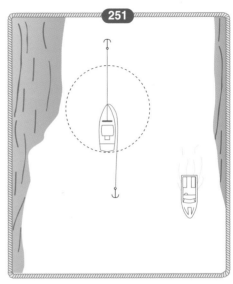

The above anchoring technique is called a "_____ _____" and is useful to reduce a boat's swing circle in tight anchorages.

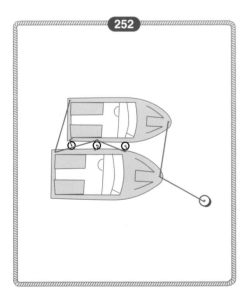

In a typical rafting arrangement, boats are cushioned by fenders and tethered by bow and stern lines, as well as a three-point spring line. Note that the stern line runs from the port cleat to the other boat's port cleat... **why**?

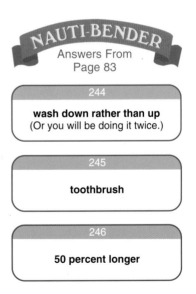

NAUTI-BENDER
Answers From
Page 83

244

wash down rather than up
(Or you will be doing it twice.)

245

toothbrush

246

50 percent longer

253

The "_____ *Device*" (Type IV PFD) is designed to be easily thrown and the seat cushion type should **not** be worn on the back as it will force the wearer's face into the water.

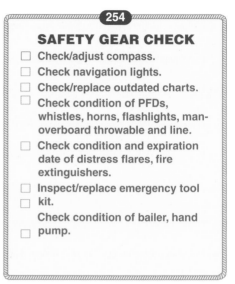

254

SAFETY GEAR CHECK

- [ ] Check/adjust compass.
- [ ] Check navigation lights.
- [ ] Check/replace outdated charts.
- [ ] Check condition of PFDs, whistles, horns, flashlights, man-overboard throwable and line.
- [ ] Check condition and expiration date of distress flares, fire extinguishers.
- [ ] Inspect/replace emergency tool kit.
- [ ] Check condition of bailer, hand pump.

What important check has been omitted from the above list?

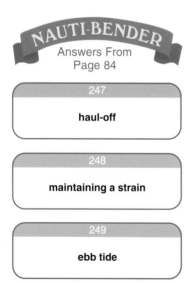

NAUTI-BENDER
Answers From
Page 84

247

haul-off

248

maintaining a strain

249

ebb tide

255

The two most important steps before getting under way, under power (vessels with gas engine(s) or propane cooking fuel), is to _____ the bilges and engine compartment for fumes and to run the engine blower for at least five minutes.

256

TRAILER

- ☐ Make sure registration is current.
- ☐ Check condition of rollers and bunks.
- ☐ Check wheel bearings for wear, pitting, and waterproof grease.
- ☐ Check bearing grease seals for leaks.
- ☐ Clean and oil the winch.
- ☐ Inspect/replace rope/cable.
- ☐ Lubricate tongue jack handle and wheel.
- ☐ Test lights, electrical connections.
- ☐ Check brakes, hydraulic fluid level.

What important check has been omitted from the above list?

257

It is good practice for every boat operating beyond VHF radio range (20 to 25 miles) to carry an ___ ___ ___ ___ ___ (EPIRB).

258

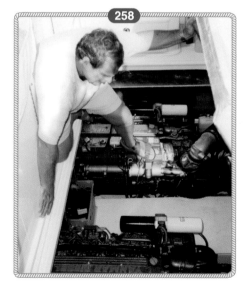

Safety Tip: Always ___ the ignition key or ___ ___ the ignition system's power source before working around the engine or propeller.

NAUTI-BENDER
Answers From
Page 85

250
light air

251
Bahamian Moor

252
This provides for a longer line, thus greater elasticity to protect from waves and wakes.

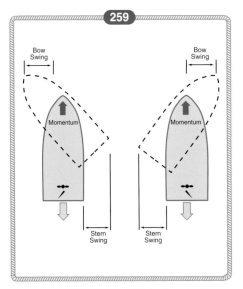

A single-screw boat (right-handed propeller) will have more stern swing when turning to the **left** or **right**.

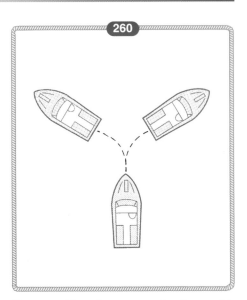

You are skippering a powerboat on a fair sea when a passenger falls overboard on the port side. You should take an immediate hard turn to the _____.

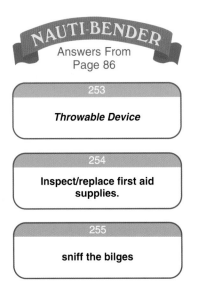

NAUTI-BENDER
Answers From Page 86

253

Throwable Device

254

Inspect/replace first aid supplies.

255

sniff the bilges

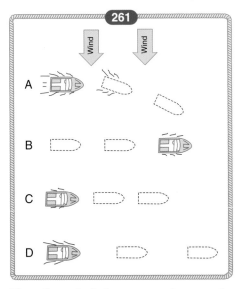

The effect of wind on exposed areas of a vessel is most noticeable when: **turning**; **backing**; **going slow ahead**; or **going full ahead**.

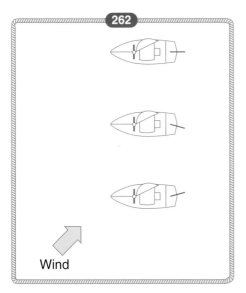

Wind

When a sailboat is in proper balance, the boat will have **no helm**, a **slight weather** or **lee helm**?

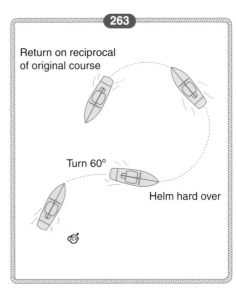

Return on reciprocal of original course

Turn 60°

Helm hard over

The "_____ Turn": the accepted method used by both power and sailboats under power to return to and rescue crew overboard.

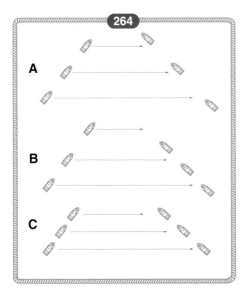

A

B

C

Cruising at a constant speed/course, you observe a vessel at two o'clock. What do the sighted bearings "**A**", "**B**", "**C**" (shown above) taken off the same fixed object on your vessel indicate?

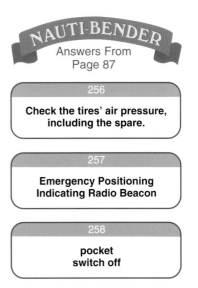

NAUTI-BENDER

Answers From
Page 87

256

Check the tires' air pressure, including the spare.

257

Emergency Positioning Indicating Radio Beacon

258

**pocket
switch off**

Pulling into a marina for the night (no hookups), you have the choice of docking port or starboard-to your neighbor. Why should you first ask the neighbor which side his **bilge pump discharge**, **generator exhaust**, or **fuel fill** is on?

Answers From Page 88

259
left

260
left (Hopefully, to keep the propeller(s) away from the victim.)

261
when backing

When docking, what determines the proper **height** and **position** of the boat's fenders?

By rigging the above shown "haul-off" to your dock, existing wharfage can be expanded by _____ boats.

When docking with non-crew, shoreside line handlers – to keep "control" (line length, surging, when the line is cleated, etc.)... pass over the _____ end of the line.

Before docking or leaving a berth, the two most important factors to consider are _____ and _____.

When docking, after considering wind/tide etc., planning the maneuver and instructing the crew... the well-prepared skipper will also have a pre-selected _____ route should it be needed.

Answers From Page 89

262

no helm

263

the *Williamson Turn*

264

A: vessel will pass ahead
B: vessel will pass astern
C: vessel on collision course

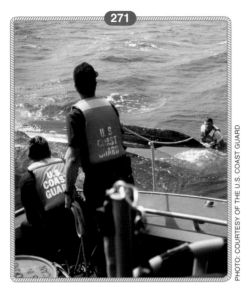

PHOTO: COURTESY OF THE U.S. COAST GUARD

In a crew-overboard situation, where should the life ring be thrown: **behind and beyond**; **to the right of**; or **in front of the victim**?

PHOTO: COURTESY OF THE U.S. COAST GUARD

In a crew-overboard situation, it is important to assume a **H**eat **E**scape **L**essening **P**osture (H.E.L.P.) or "fetal" position, since _____ percent of the body's heat is lost from the head.

NAUTI-BENDER
Answers From Page 90

265

generator exhaust (a potential carbon monoxide threat... dock on the opposite side.)

266

height: height of the dock position: docking maneuver planned

267

two boats

PHOTO: COURTESY OF THE U.S. COAST GUARD

If your flares are inoperative, used up, or not available, and other emergency distress signals (fog horn sounded continuously, gun fire, smoky fire, etc.) don't work... try pointing a camera and activating the _____ to attract attention.

PHOTO: COURTESY OF THE U.S. COAST GUARD

The key to a successful rescue in a crew-overboard situation is : (A) **good communication**; (B) **a good crew**; (C) **the proper equipment made easily accessible**; (D) **regularly scheduled drills**.

PHOTO: COURTESY OF BOSTON WHALER BOATS

If one of the four most common boating emergencies: _____; _____; _____; or _____-_____ happens on your vessel... will you and your crew be prepared?

PHOTO: COURTESY OF THE U.S. COAST GUARD

How long are distress flares approved for: **24 months**; **36 months**; or **42 months**?

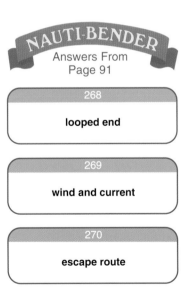

NAUTI-BENDER
Answers From
Page 91

268
looped end

269
wind and current

270
escape route

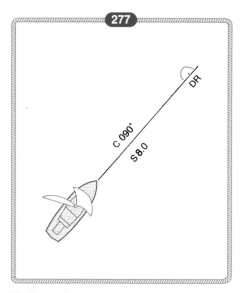

You're underway on 090°T at 8 knots. After two hours, you are on your track line but two miles behind your DR. What is the set and drift of the current?

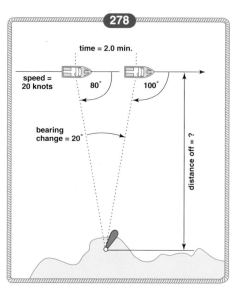

Using the "angle = speed" method shown above, determine the "distance off" where distance off = time.

NAUTI-BENDER
Answers From
Page 92

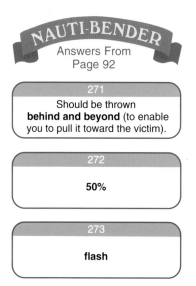

271
Should be thrown **behind and beyond** (to enable you to pull it toward the victim).

272

50%

273

flash

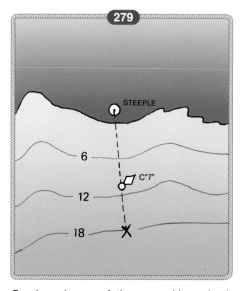

Coming abeam of the can with a depth reading of 18 feet... could you assume that you were approximately at point "**X**" shown above?

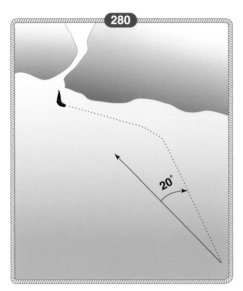

In unfamiliar or unbuoyed waters, or in fog; trying to navigate to a river or harbor entrance without GPS or Loran-C is tricky. To eliminate confusion, overshoot the _____ course and then follow the shoreline until you find the entrance.

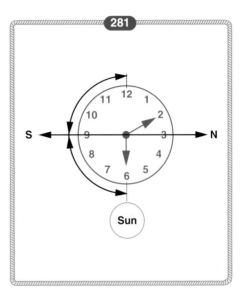

Approximate direction can be determined by a line midway between the hour hand and 12 o'clock indicating south in the _____ hemisphere and north in the _____ hemisphere.

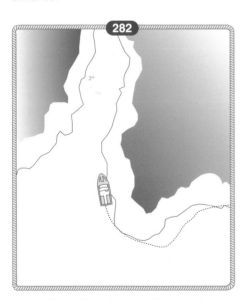

Navigating with only a depth sounder can be accomplished by "sounding" a course that follows an appropriate "depth _____ line" on the associated chart... **True** or **False**?

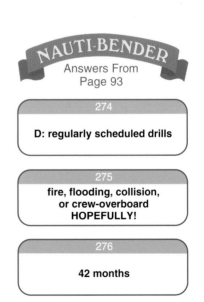

NAUTI-BENDER
Answers From
Page 93

274

D: regularly scheduled drills

275

fire, flooding, collision, or crew-overboard HOPEFULLY!

276

42 months

The Color of the Sky is a Good Weather Predictor: Bright yellow at sunset – **wind** or **rain**; pale yellow at sunset – **wind** or **rain**; dark blue during the day – **wind** or **rain**; light blue during the day – **good** or **bad** weather.

The wind's direction is said to "veer" when it shifts **clockwise** or **counter-clockwise** (typically after a front passes). The true wind is said to "_____" when its speed increases.

NAUTI-BENDER
Answers From
Page 94

277
270° at 1 knot

278
2.0 nautical miles

279
Probably not ± feet for tide, and + feet for depth of the transducer.

Using a Barometer to Predict the Weather: Rapid rise – _____ weather; slow rise – _____ weather; alternate rise and fall – _____ weather; rapid fall – _____ and _____.

PHOTO BY: PAT PIPER, ANNAPOLIS, MD

When a high tide exceeds average height, will the following low tide be **higher** or **lower** than average?

PHOTO BY: JOHN SNYDER, NORTH CONWAY, NH

The color of an evening sky can be a good indicator of the next day's weather. A yellow sunset typically means **strong** or **light** winds, especially at midday.

Wind changes direction either by "_____" or "_____". When these shifts occur, it is a good indicator of impending weather changes.

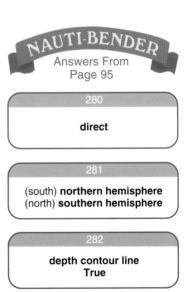

NAUTI-BENDER
Answers From
Page 95

280
direct

281
(south) **northern hemisphere**
(north) **southern hemisphere**

282
depth contour line
True

Boarding a Sailboat from the Pier: As close as possible to the point of maximum beam, put one foot on the gunwale and grab onto a **shroud**, **stanchion**, or **lifeline** and haul yourself aboard.

Flag Etiquette: In the strictest sense, pleasure vessels that are "documented" are **required** to fly the _____ _____ while in U.S. territorial waters.

NAUTI-BENDER

Answers From
Page 96

283
wind **rain** **wind, good weather**

284
clockwise **freshen**

285
unsettled weather; fair weather; unsettled weather; gale and rain

PHOTO: COURTESY OF ACR ELECTRONICS, INC.

An EPIRB can send a signal as far as _____ miles, alerting land stations, rescue vessels and passing _____ that an emergency exists, and will lead searchers to the distress scene.

1

2

3

PHOTO: COURTESY OF THE U.S. COAST GUARD

Identify the organizations that the flags shown above represent. Which of the organizations has law enforcement authority?

293

Boaters' Clothes: _____ colors when it's hot; _____ colors when it's cold and _____ colors for heavy weather (in the rare event you should fall overboard).

294

PHOTO: COURTESY OF THE U.S. COAST GUARD

After colliding with another vessel, the penalty for failing to give aid without reasonable cause is _____ year(s) imprisonment or a $_____ fine.

NAUTI-BENDER
Answers From
Page 97

286

lower

287

strong winds

288

veering or backing

PHOTO: COURTESY OF TIARA YACHTS, BY FOREST JOHNSON

Running into heavy, closely-spaced, steep-sided waves (beam or quartering sea) may be dangerous and uncomfortable. In this situation, what corrective maneuver is advisable?

On a power vessel equipped with a single prop, propeller action alone will have the most directional control when the engine is full _____.

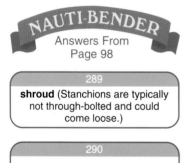

NAUTI-BENDER
Answers From Page 98

289
shroud (Stanchions are typically not through-bolted and could come loose.)

290
the yacht ensign

291
200 miles aircraft

PHOTO: COURTESY OF TIARA YACHTS

While going ahead on twin engines (rudders amidships) your port engine stalls. To continue on course you should: (A) **apply right rudder**; (B) **apply left rudder**; (C) **keep rudders amidships**; or (D) **increase engine speed**.

PHOTO: COURTESY OF THE U.S. COAST GUARD

Many boating accidents occur (especially at night or in fog) when a Skipper, unfamiliar with the _____ lights scheme, tries to pass between a tug (which may be utilizing up to a 1200-foot hawser) and its tow.

Running with a heavy following sea, you sense that the boat is being pushed towards a broach. You should turn the wheel hard over in the direction that the stern is heading and **apply full power** or **decrease acceleration**.

PHOTO: COURTESY OF TIARA YACHTS, BY FOREST JOHNSON

NAUTI-BENDER
Answers From
Page 99

292
1: C.G. Auxiliary, 2: U.S.C.G.
(has law enforcement authority)
3: U.S. Power Squadron

293
hot: white or light colors
cold: dark colors
heavy weather: bright colors

294
two years imprisonment
or a $1,000 fine

Which of the following sea conditions is the most difficult and offers the most uncomfortable ride in heavy weather: **a headsea; from broad on the bow**; **a quartering sea**; **a beam sea**; or **a following sea**?

301

PHOT: BY CARLO BORLENGHI

A "following sea" comes from astern in the same direction as the boat is heading... a "_____ sea" is just the opposite. "Cross" or "confused" seas are irregular with components from two or more _____ .

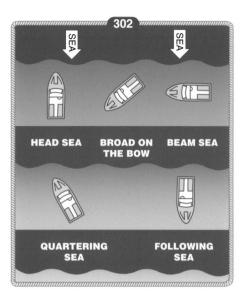

302

SEA   SEA

HEAD SEA   **BROAD ON THE BOW**   **BEAM SEA**

QUARTERING SEA   **FOLLOWING SEA**

In the above graphic, which sea condition descriptor(s) have been mislabeled?

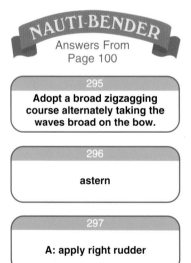

NAUTI-BENDER
Answers From
Page 100

295

Adopt a broad zigzagging course alternately taking the waves broad on the bow.

296

astern

297

A: apply right rudder

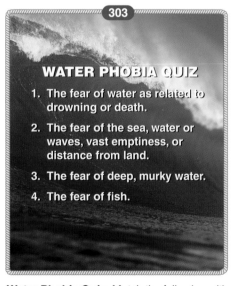

303

WATER PHOBIA QUIZ

1. The fear of water as related to drowning or death.

2. The fear of the sea, water or waves, vast emptiness, or distance from land.

3. The fear of deep, murky water.

4. The fear of fish.

Water Phobia Quiz: Match the following with the definitions offered above: (**A**) Thalassophobia; (**B**) Ichthyophobia; (**C**) Hydrophobia; and (**D**) Bathophobia.

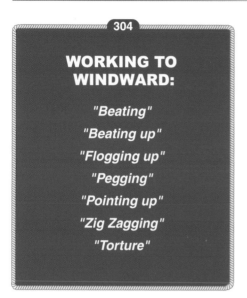

304

WORKING TO WINDWARD:

"Beating"

"Beating up"

"Flogging up"

"Pegging"

"Pointing up"

"Zig Zagging"

"Torture"

Which of the above terms does not mean "working to windward"?

305

PHOTO: COURTESY OF PURSUIT BOATS

While underway at cruising speed, you observe some cute obstacles dead ahead and shift the engine(s) into full reverse. The distance that your boat will travel until it is dead in the water is referred to as "_____ _____".

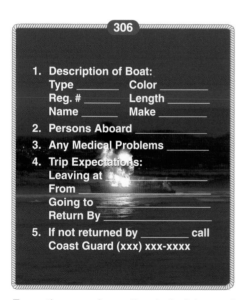

306

1. **Description of Boat:**
   Type _____ Color _____
   Reg. # _____ Length _____
   Name _____ Make _____
2. **Persons Aboard** _____
3. **Any Medical Problems** _____
4. **Trip Expectations:**
   Leaving at _____
   From _____
   Going to _____
   Return By _____
5. **If not returned by** _____ **call**
   Coast Guard (xxx) xxx-xxxx

Every time you leave the dock, it is good practice to leave a "_____ plan" with someone ashore.

NAUTI-BENDER
Answers From
Page 101

298

navigational lights scheme

299

**apply full power
until the boat straightens out**

300

**A quartering sea causes
rolling/yawing and has the
most effect on your steering.**

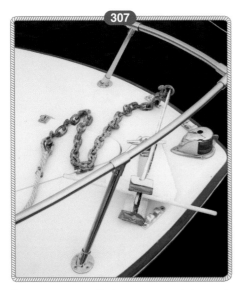

"_____ _____" is a general term to describe the anchor, rode, fittings, etc. used to anchor a boat.

You're installing a new halyard line... how long should it be?

Lashing mooring pendants at regular intervals with "_____ stuff" will avoid tangles and strength-diminishing kinks.

Nylon lines are weakened by dyeing – **True** or **False**?

Nylon rope makes an excellent dock line because of its _____. This unique characteristic cushions surges from waves or wakes in rough anchorages.

PHOTO: COURTESY OF THE U.S. COAST GUARD

Nylon line has a working elasticity of up to _____% under load.

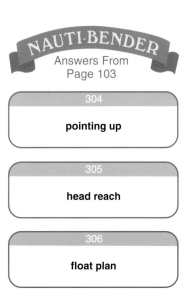

NAUTI-BENDER
Answers From
Page 103

304
pointing up

305
head reach

306
float plan

A powerboat not making way in restricted visibility should sound _____ prolonged blasts every two minutes.

If underway in fog, a power vessel should sound a prolonged blast at least once every _____ minutes.

Answers From
Page 104

307
Ground tackle

308
In general, 2¼ times the mast's height will be enough.

309
small stuff

In fog, a sailing vessel should sound a _____ blast followed by two _____ blasts every two minutes.

A bell is used to sound a fog signal for vessels at _____ or _____.

While cruising in fog, you hear a signal ahead (a long blast followed by two short blasts) indicating a vessel is engaged in: **fishing**; **towing** or **pushing**; **sailing**; or **all of the above**.

In fog, while cruising in heavily congested areas, it is good practice to _____ your engine(s) at regular intervals and listen for fog signals.

NAUTI-BENDER
Answers From
Page 105

310
True (The strongest nylon lines, given the same diameter, are white.)

311
elasticity (It also helps to double or triple the lines... create a spiderweb.)

312

25%

When winterizing your engine (diesel or gasoline), it is good practice to run the engine without a coolant water source until no water comes out of the exhaust – **True** or **False**?

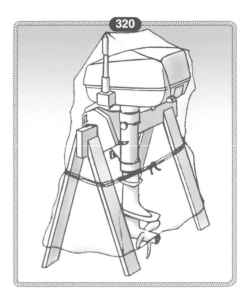

Outboard Motor Storage: Motors should always be stored vertically so the coolant water remaining in the system can drain. **Always** or **never** wrap the motor in plastic with duct tape to protect it over the winter.

NAUTI-BENDER
Answers From
Page 106

313
two prolonged blasts

314
2 minutes
(More often if in close proximity to other vessels.)

315
prolonged blast followed by two short blasts

PHOTO: COURTESY OF ALDEN YACHTS

Many yachtsmen keep excess mooring lines looking neat on the deck by laying out the line in tight successive circles with the "bitter end" in the center... this practice is referred to as "_____".

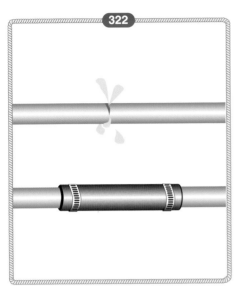

322

Having trouble slipping on a tight hose or getting hose-type chafing gear slipped over a line? The difficulty may be eliminated by lubricating the items with liquid _____ _____.

323

PHOTO: COURTESY OF TIARA YACHTS, BY FOREST JOHNSON

Diesel Engine Performance: Approximately 90% of engine problems emanate from _____ or _____ in the fuel.

324

In a salt water environment, to prolong a vessel's diesel or gasoline engine's life and minimize repairs, it is a good practice to "_____" the engine with fresh water on a regular basis.

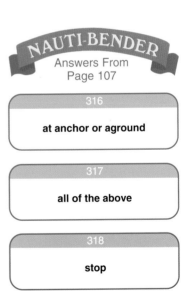

NAUTI-BENDER
Answers From
Page 107

316

at anchor or aground

317

all of the above

318

stop

A cylindrical buoy, tapered at the top and typically red in color is called a "_____" buoy.

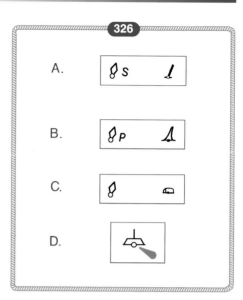

What do the chart symbols shown in "**A**", "**B**", "**C**", and "**D**" above indicate to the navigator?

NAUTI-BENDER
Answers From
Page 108

319
True – prevents freezing
(Even better, run antifreeze through the system.)

320
never wrap motor (Condensation will collect and corrode the electrical system.)

321
flemishing

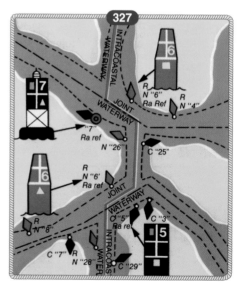

Red, Right, Returning Is the Rule: However, the government's definition of returning may differ from yours. Heading home to Annapolis from Fort Lauderdale on the Intracoastal Waterway, you would keep red to right... **right**?

328

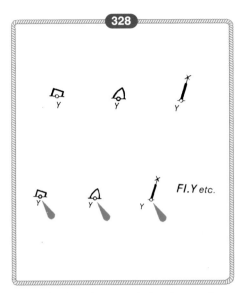

Fl.Y etc.

What do the chart symbols shown above indicate to the navigator?

329

Entering from sea, you encounter a red and green horizontally-banded buoy. The top band is red indicating the preferred channel is with the buoy to the **port** or **starboard side** of your boat.

330

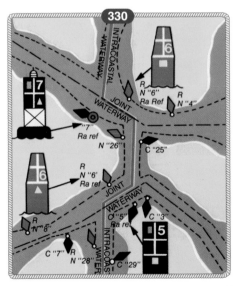

You are entering an east coast port and see a buoy with a yellow triangle painted on it, indicating... ?

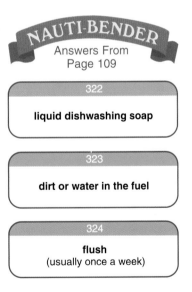

NAUTI-BENDER
Answers From
Page 109

322

liquid dishwashing soap

323

dirt or water in the fuel

324

flush
(usually once a week)

Second-priority urgent communications concerning the safety of a ship, an aircraft, other vessel, or person in sight, or on board, should be preceded by "_____-_____" (repeated three times).

VHF Communications: Which of the following channels should be utilized for distress, safety, and calling transmissions: **13**; **16**; **22A**; **24**; **27**; **71**; or **72**?

NAUTI-BENDER
Answers From
Page 110

325
nun buoy

326
A: *spar or spindlebuoy*;
B: *pillarbuoy*;   C: *barrelbuoy*;
D: *superbuoy*

327
wrong – Keep red on the right going south on the Intercoastal Waterway.

Generally speaking, the **longer** or **shorter** the VHF antenna, the greater its gain or effective range.

VHF radios have a working range of between _____ to _____ miles in ideal conditions.

Proper procedural words to be used during VHF radio communications include the following, except: "**this is**"; "**come back**"; "**say again**"; "**over**"; "**roger**"; or "**over and out**".

PHOTO: COURTESY OF THE U.S. COAST GUARD

Only when there is imminent danger of loss of life or vessel, should the universal emergency call "_____, _____, _____", be radioed.

NAUTI-BENDER
Answers From Page 111

328
special marks (not primarily to assist navigation, but to indicate special features)

329
starboard side

330
You are in the vicinity of the Intracoastal Waterway.

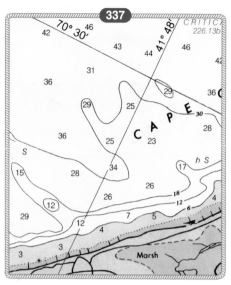

Horizontal or vertical lines on nautical charts are called meridians of longitude and are angular measurements of distance _____ or _____ of the prime meridian located at _____, England.

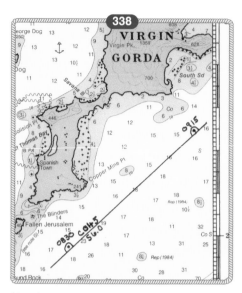

How far would you travel in 45 minutes if you were steaming at 6 knots? What does the anchor in the upper left hand corner of the chart shown above indicate to the navigator?

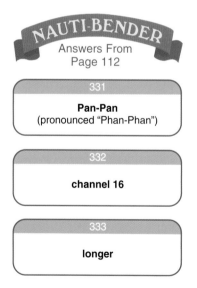

NAUTI-BENDER
Answers From
Page 112

331

Pan-Pan
(pronounced "Phan-Phan")

332

channel 16

333

longer

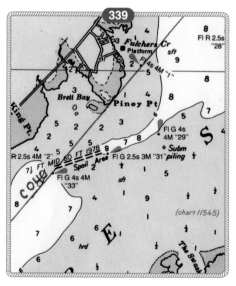

Assuming your vessel draws three feet, when should you schedule your sightseeing trip to Piney Point?

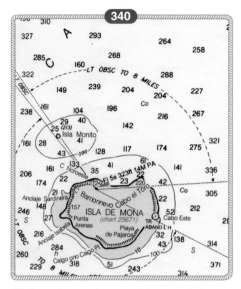

While underway in a small boat at night, you intermittently observe a light (ISLA de MONA lighthouse) on the horizon. The approximate distance to the lighthouse would be **15**, **20**, or **25** miles.

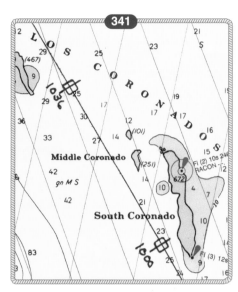

The Six Minute Rule: States that a vessel will travel one-tenth her speed (in distance) in six minutes. Applying this rule... how far will a vessel cruising at 10 knots travel in 36 minutes?

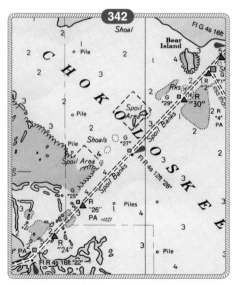

"PA" printed adjacent to a navigational aid on a chart means its position is _____.

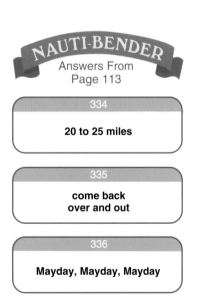

NAUTI-BENDER
Answers From
Page 113

334
20 to 25 miles

335
**come back
over and out**

336
Mayday, Mayday, Mayday

343

RETRIEVING THE BOAT

1. Hook the winch cable to the back of the trailer.
2. Back trailer squarely into the water.
3. Put transmission in park and put emergency brake on.
4. Chock the car's tires.
5. Connect the cable to the bow eye and winch the boat onto the trailer.
6. Using low gear, slowly pull the trailer up the ramp.
7. Secure all loose gear and the boat to the trailer.
8. Remove drain plugs.

The above offers a procedure for retrieving the boat from the ramp. Why is it suggested that the winch cable be hooked to the back of the trailer?

344

Small boats don't have to be going fast to fly a long distance after hitting something solid (another boat, big log, rock, etc). For example, if you were cruising at 24 mph and hit something, the boat could fly **20**, **40**, or **60** feet.

Answers From Page 114

337
vertical lines
east or west
Greenwich, England

338
4.5 nautical miles
anchorage (large vessels)

339
at high tide

345

AVOID

1. Overloading, poor trim, over-powering.
2. Fast turns in rough water.
3. Failure to look out for obstacles.
4. Departing, or getting caught in rough weather.
5. Standing up in a moving boat.
6. Riding on the bow.
7. Leaky fuel system.
8. Going too far offshore.
9. Overindulgence in alcohol.

The above lists the major causes of boating _____ which should be avoided if possible.

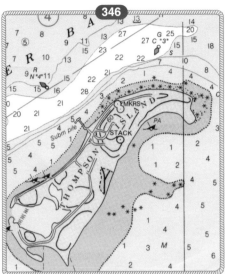

346

Cruising close to Thompson Island, could you assume that the presence of numerous lobster pots indicates water depths that could be safely navigated (your boat draws 4½')?

347

LEAVING A BOAT UNATTENDED

1. **Check battery level.**

2. **Secure all unnecessary power.**

3. **Shut all seacocks.**

4. **Disconnect propane bottle(s).**

5. **Check bilge pumps.**

6. **Shut off fuel supply.**

Whether in a slip or on a mooring, it is good practice to always "_____" the boat in a proper fashion.

348

FLOAT PLAN

1. **Description of Boat:**
   - Type _____   Color _____
   - Reg.# _____   Length _____
   - Name _____   Make _____

2. **Persons Aboard** _____

3. **Any Medical Problems** _____

4. **Trip Expectations:**
   - Leaving at _____
   - From _____
   - Going to _____
   - Return By _____

5. **If not returned by** _____ **call Coast Guard (xxx) xxx-xxxx.**

Before getting under way, your checklist should include: **fuel**; **lubrication** and **bilge levels**; **weather forecast**; **leaving a float plan with a responsible person on shore**; or **all of the above**?

NAUTI-BENDER
Answers From Page 115

340

1.14 x √Ht. of lighthouse =
1.14 x √323 = 20.4 nm

341

6 nautical miles
$10 \times \frac{36}{60} = 6$

342

position is approximate

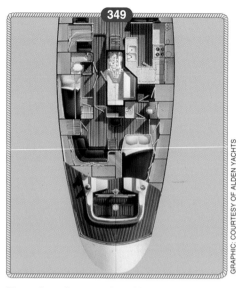

349

GRAPHIC: COURTESY OF ALDEN YACHTS

Every boat has a sole, which is the _____ of the cabin or the cockpit.

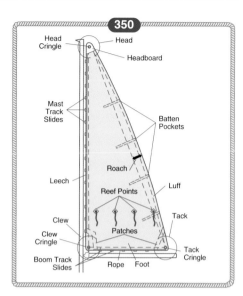

350

Head Cringle · Head
Headboard
Mast Track Slides
Batten Pockets
Roach
Leech · Luff
Reef Points
Clew · Tack
Clew Cringle · Patches
Boom Track Slides · Tack Cringle
Rope · Foot

In the above diagram, which sail descriptors have been transposed?

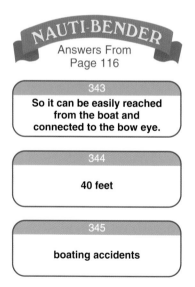

NAUTI-BENDER
Answers From
Page 116

343
So it can be easily reached from the boat and connected to the bow eye.

344
40 feet

345
boating accidents

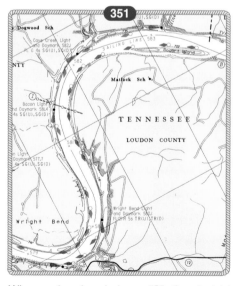

351

Dogwood Sch
Cove Creek Light and Daymark 582J
Fl G 4s SG(U),SG(D)
NTY
Bacon Light and Daymark 584
4s SG(U),SG(D)
Matlock Sch
TENNESSEE
LOUDON COUNTY
Wright Bend Light and Daymark 580J
Fl R 5s TR(U),TR(D)
Wright Bend

When a river bends in an "S", the straight section between the curves is called a "_____". On major rivers these are marked by "ranges" or directional lights.

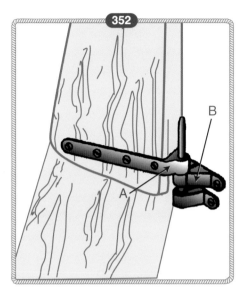

A rudder fitting referred to as the "_____" ("**A**" shown above) is the eye socket into which the "_____" ("**B**" shown above) is slipped to form a hinge about which the rudder pivots.

The "_____" is a storage space at the stern of a small boat, sometimes utilized to house auxiliary power in sailing vessels.

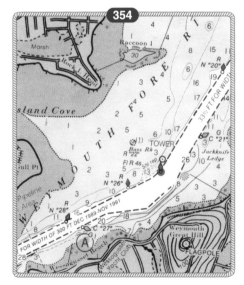

Nautical charts utilize _____ lettering to label all information about objects that are not affected by tide or current.

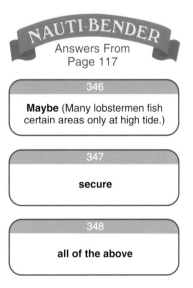

NAUTI-BENDER
Answers From
Page 117

346

Maybe (Many lobstermen fish certain areas only at high tide.)

347

secure

348

all of the above

355

PHOTO: COURTESY OF BOSTON WHALER BOATS, BY MIKE FULLER

In waterskiing parlance: if one is "skiing 15 off"... what does this mean?

356

OK, stainless steel is the best metal for cleats and deck hardware, but it comes in many grades. How do you check... (A) **with a magnet**; (B) **by how shiny it is**; or (C) **by tapping with a brass key**?

NAUTI-BENDER
Answers From
Page 118

349

floor

350

"Tack" should be "Clew" and vice versa.

351

crossing

357

PHOTO: COURTESY OF THE U.S. COAST GUARD

Nautical Trivia: What is the U.S. Coast Guard's motto... **"semper fidelis"**, **"protect and save"**, or **"semper partus"**?

A "modified-V hull" requires more power than a flat-bottomed boat, but less than a "full _____-V hull" design.

Tides go in and out... not on this planet! _____ go in and out and _____ go up and down.

Because fuel gauges on small boats are notoriously inaccurate or nonexistent, many Skippers install an auxiliary tank or carry a "_____-_____-_____" portable fuel tank.

NAUTI-BENDER
Answers From
Page 119

352

A: gudgeon
B: pintle

353

lazarette

354

straight or block lettering

Engine Fire Procedure: Head the boat **into** or **with** the wind; shut down the engine and secure the fuel supply; then extinguish the fire with: **water**; a **Type B**; or a **Type C** fire extinguisher.

It is good practice to have an In Case of Emergency Card (should the Skipper become incapacitated) located by the helm. The card should list simple instructions, in non-nautical terms **on how to**...

NAUTI-BENDER
Answers From
Page 120

355

Their tow rope is 15' shorter than standard length or 60'.

356

A: with a magnet
(The less it sticks...
the better it is.)

357

semper partus
(always ready)

Believe it or not, lowering or raising the anchor or picking up a mooring are prime opportunities to _____ _____.

Boarding a boat, while carrying gear in both hands, can be dangerous. How can it be done safely?

In the event of a fire emergency, the first steps should include: manning the fire extinguishers; securing power (if an electrical fire); and maneuvering the boat so the fire is on the *lee* or **windward** side.

You request a Courtesy Marine Examination from the Coast Guard Auxiliary. The inspector finds that your MSD's Y-valve is in the "holding tank position" but can easily be switched to "overboard". Does your boat **pass** or **fail**?

NAUTI-BENDER
Answers From
Page 121

358

deep-V

359

Currents go in and out tides go up and down.

360

get-you-home

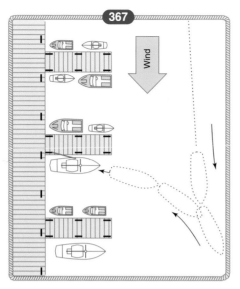

Docking in a leeward berth (assuming good reverse control)... back in smartly and work _____ slow on the after bow spring until all other lines are secured.

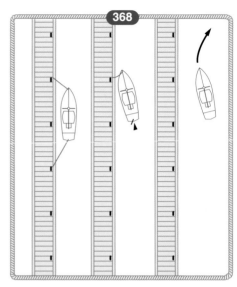

The unberthing procedure shown above would be proper with the wind and current coming from: **ahead**, **the starboard beam**, or **behind**.

NAUTI-BENDER
Answers From
Page 122

361

**head the boat into the wind
Type B fire extinguisher**

362

**stop, anchor, call for help,
determine the boat's position,
location of first aid kit, etc.**

363

fall overboard
(slippery decks, leaning over too
far, wave/wake motion, etc.)

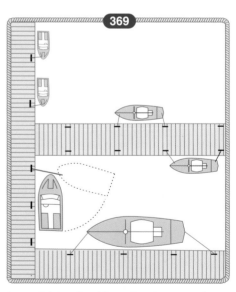

In a tight unberthing situation, as shown above, utilizing a bow spring line with the engine slow _____ and with hard _____ rudder is quite useful.

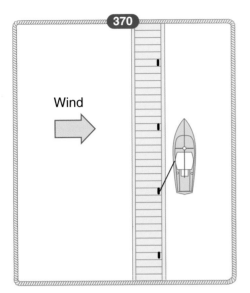

Single-Handed Docking: To hold the boat against the pier while securing the rest of the lines, utilize a spring from the winch or amidship's cleat with the engine working slow _____ and the rudder hard _____.

"Walking" sideways with twin-engines: apply hard _____ rudder with alternating short bursts of power forward and astern on the _____ engine until you reach the pier; then use the _____ engine to bring the bow or stern in.

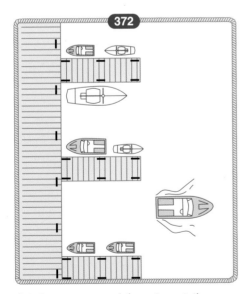

A twin-screw vessel (counter-rotating propellers) with the rudders amidships, and with both engines backing... will back **in a fairly straight line**; **to port**; or **to starboard**.

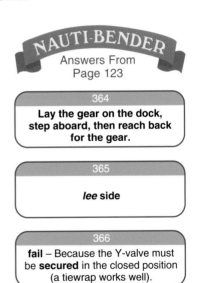

NAUTI-BENDER
Answers From
Page 123

364

Lay the gear on the dock, step aboard, then reach back for the gear.

365

lee side

366

fail – Because the Y-valve must be **secured** in the closed position (a tiewrap works well).

The National Marine Fisheries Service recommends that all vessels maintain a distance of _____ yards from all whales and at least _____ yards from Right whales, which are protected.

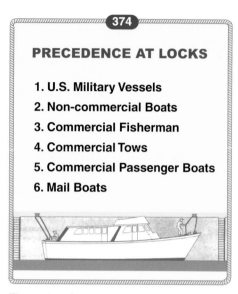

PRECEDENCE AT LOCKS

1. **U.S. Military Vessels**
2. **Non-commercial Boats**
3. **Commercial Fisherman**
4. **Commercial Tows**
5. **Commercial Passenger Boats**
6. **Mail Boats**

The order of lock precedence shown above has been rearranged. What is the correct order?

Answers From Page 124

367
ahead slow

368
from behind

369
engine slow astern hard left rudder

PHOTO: COURTESY OF THE U.S. COAST GUARD

Small boats by law, must have a PFD: (A) **for the stated maximum number of passengers**; (B) **for each person on board**; (C) **for each child (to be worn at all times)**; (D) **and a "throwable" Type IV**; or (E) **all of the above**.

376

RIGHT-OF-WAY RANKINGS

A. Power-driven vessels

B. Vessels restricted in ability to maneuver

C. Vessels engaged in fishing

D. Vessels not under command

E. Sailing vessels

Per the navigation rules, when two vessels are in close proximity, one vessel (usually the less maneuverable) has the right of way... **list the above in the order of the highest to the lowest ranking**.

377

PHOTO: COURTESY OF THE U.S. COAST GUARD

U.S. Coast Guard Navigation Rules state that every vessel shall maintain a proper _____-_____ at **all** times in any visibility.

378

PHOTO: COURTESY OF ACR ELECTRONICS, INC

EPIRBs have a readiness test switch to check for proper operation. Tests should be conducted for _____ second(s) during the first _____ minutes of the hour (reserved for testing) to avoid false alarms.

NAUTI-BENDER
Answers From
Page 125

370
slow ahead
rudder hard right
(or away from the dock)

371
hard left rudder
port engine
starboard engine

372
in a fairly straight line

PHOTO: COURTESY OF PURSUIT BOATS, BY FOREST JOHNSON

Rainbow Reading – A rainbow is created by the refraction of sunlight in drops of rain in the air: "rainbow to windward, _____ falls the day"; "rainbow to leeward, _____ runs away".

The shape of clouds can be a good weather indicator. Soft, delicate clouds during the day usually mean _____ weather; hard-edged, wispy clouds during the day usually mean _____.

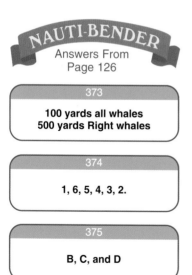

NAUTI-BENDER
Answers From
Page 126

373
100 yards all whales
500 yards Right whales

374
1, 6, 5, 4, 3, 2.

375
B, C, and D

Storm Predictor:
1. A lot of rain before the wind... typically means?
2. A sharp gust first, then rain... typically means?

Mariners use a scale of 0 to 12 to describe the wind's force, a system developed by, and named after, British Rear Admiral, Sir Francis _____.

PHOTO: COURTESY OF WALKER MANGUM, BY WALKER MANGUM

Rainbow Reading: A rainbow in the **morning**; at **midday**; or **at evening** indicates: **the storm is over**; **an approaching storm**; or **unsettled weather** – match the times with the indicator.

Sound travels further when the air has **higher** or **lower** humidity.

NAUTI-BENDER
Answers From
Page 127

376
D, B, C, E, A

377
look-out
(by sight and hearing)

378
**one second
five minutes**

The centerboard **does not** have to be down when: **beating**; **running**; or **reaching**.

In an emergency, diesel engines can be run completely underwater, provided the **fuel supply**, **battery**, or **air intake** is above water.

If your boat has gone aground on a falling tide... the best action you can take is to set out a "_____" anchor.

In heavy weather, a boat should be headed slightly _____ into the waves.

Hard-chined sailboats sail **faster** or **slower** with the chines buried.

For safe waterskiing it is recommended that a _____ foot wide, unobstructed "ski corridor" at least _____ to _____ feet long be utilized.

NAUTI-BENDER
Answers From
Page 129

382

Sir Francis Beaufort

383

**morning: approaching storm
midday: unsettled weather
evening: the storm is over**

384

higher ("When sound travels far and wide, a stormy day will like betide.")

391

How can you help prevent the paint/varnish peeling, fading, and drying out on one side of the boat while storing it **on land** and **afloat**?

392

Heading into the dock at low tide, you note your outboard's "tell-tale" has stopped spitting. What's wrong? The hole has probably been clogged with sand. To clear it, insert an _____ _____ and spin it.

393

You notice that your boat's sacrificial anodes are getting a corrosive-looking white scale on them... is this a **good** or **bad** thing? Anode life can be extended by cleaning them with a wire brush (up to three times) before replacing them.

PHOTO: COURTESY OF THE U.S. COAST GUARD

When servicing your engine(s), special care should be exercised not to discharge oil or other pollutants into the waterways. A single quart of oil can cover an area equivalent to nearly _____ football fields.

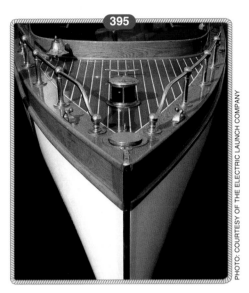

PHOTO: COURTESY OF THE ELECTRIC LAUNCH COMPANY

When "bedding" hardware on your boat, **snug** the fasteners just enough to form a continuous bead of sealant around the fitting. **Crank** down on them only after the sealant has "cured" for at least _____ hours.

Once shrink-wrap has been fitted to your boat, it can be reused year after year – **True** or **False**?

NAUTI-BENDER
Answers From
Page 131

388
slightly angled into the waves

389
slower

390
200 foot wide 2,000 to 3,000 feet long

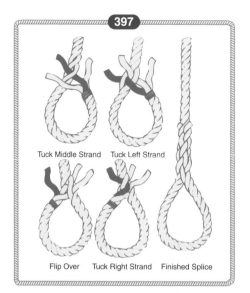

Tuck Middle Strand   Tuck Left Strand

Flip Over   Tuck Right Strand   Finished Splice

To make custom length dock lines and/or save money, splice the *eyes* as shown above. Note: the tucks are made **against** or **with** the *lay* of the *standing part*.

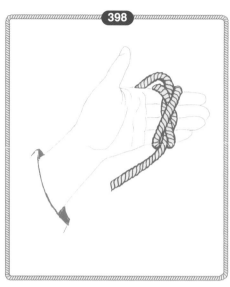

The "_____" knot is useful for gripping round objects; however, it is difficult to untie.

Answers From
Page 132

391
Land: position the boat on a north/south axis. **Afloat**: turn the boat end-for-end regularly.

392
allen wrench (or a rigid piece of wire)

393
This is a good thing. (Corrosion is attacking the anodes instead of your engine.)

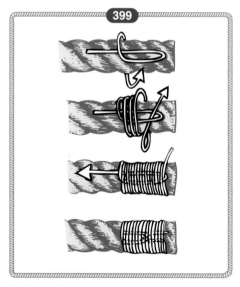

To keep lines neat and to prevent unraveling, the ends should be "_____". Make enough turns to at least equal the rope's diameter, going no closer than 3/8's of an inch to the bitter end.

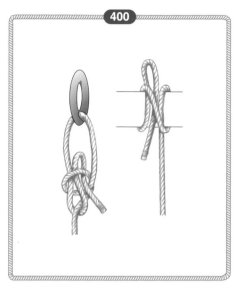

400

"_____" hitches and knots are useful in temporary situations and can be untied quickly, even under load.

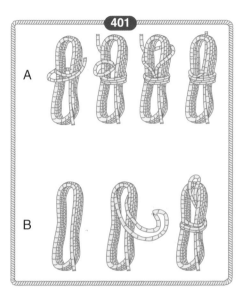

401

A

B

Halyards and lines should be routinely coiled in a similar fashion for use in a hurry or at night. "**A**" shown above illustrates coiling a line for _____ and "**B**" for _____.

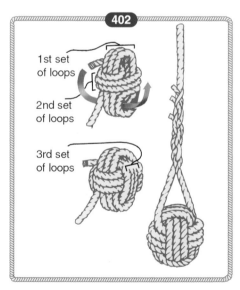

402

1st set of loops

2nd set of loops

3rd set of loops

By tying a *monkey fist* (as shown above) to the end of a heaving line, accuracy and distance will be improved. Use a series of three loops and finish off as you would an "_____" splice.

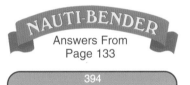

NAUTI-BENDER

Answers From
Page 133

394

three

395

24 hours (One hour for silicone)
– turn nuts only so as not to break the bolt's seal.

396

False
(The only thing that may be reusable is the zipper door.)

When departing a fore- and aft-mooring, tie the _____ together for easy retrieval when returning.

When tying up to a pier (rough, dirty, or stone walls), use a sacrificial "_____ _____" (as shown above) to protect fenders and the boat.

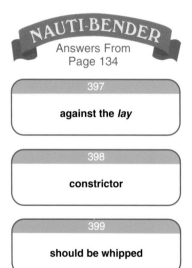

NAUTI-BENDER
Answers From
Page 134

397

against the _lay_

398

constrictor

399

should be whipped

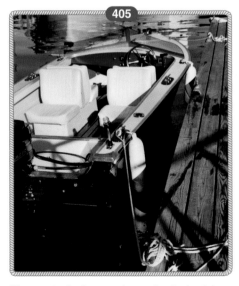

The vessel shown above is docked bow into a tidal flow or current. Utilization of which dock line would have prevented the bow from being pushed in?

If the boat manufacturer didn't install a cleat amidships on your boat... you may want to consider adding one. This addition would prove useful for "_____-_____" docking maneuvers and departures in strong wind current situations.

When docking with a strong wind or current directly abeam, you must anticipate that the **bow** or **stern** will fall off first.

NAUTI-BENDER
Answers From
Page 135

400
Slippery hitches and knots

401
stowing **hanging**

402
eye **splice** (Hint: to make the knot float, insert a hollow rubber ball.)

At your regular slip, arrivals/departures can be expedited by rigging permanent dock lines (correct length, etc.) with the **bitter end** or **loop** secured to the dock.

PHOTO: COURTESY OF PURSUIT BOATS, BY FOREST JOHNSON

Lighthouses that flash alternating lights of different colors have two ranges of visibility – one for white and another **25%**, **40%**, or **50%** shorter for red or green.

A tug pushing a barge down the Mississippi River would measure the trip in _____ miles.

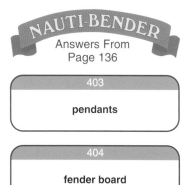

Answers From
Page 136

403
pendants

404
fender board

405
forward quarter spring line

What is the distance to the horizon for a mariner with a "height-of-eye" of nine feet (i.e., nine feet above the water's surface)?

Determining Distance Off by Visibility of Details: From approximately _____ miles individual windows of houses are distinguishable; from approximately _____ to _____ miles you will be able to see a beach.

The apparent wind speed will be zero when: the true wind is from dead **ahead** or **astern** and equals the _____ speed.

Before getting under way, your Loran-C or GPS receiver should be checked for accuracy. Save the waypoint at your launching ramp or slip. When checked, the distance should be between 0.0 to _____ miles.

NAUTI-BENDER
Answers From
Page 137

406
spring-line docking maneuvers

407
bow

408
bitter end
(Then the *eyes* can simply be slipped on or off.)

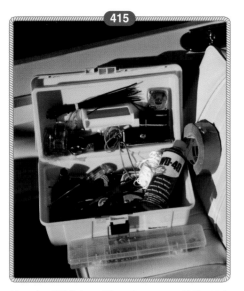

Nautical Trivia: After duct tape, WD-40 is second on the list of a well-stocked tool kit. But what does WD-40 stand for?

Documented vessels are required to display the vessel's name in three locations: port/starboard sides and the transom (also, hailing port on the transom) – **True** or **False**.

PHOTO: COURTESY OF ALDEN YACHTS

NAUTI-BENDER
Answers From
Page 138

409

25%

410

statute miles
(5,280 feet/mile)

411

Formula: 1.17 X √HE
(1.17 X √9 = 3.51 miles)

Maneuvering around a sea of lobster pots is sometimes difficult... especially at night or in fog. If you normally cruise in an area active in lobstering or crabbing, installing "line _____" on the shaft(s) may be the solution.

On a sailboat with auxiliary power, the propeller can induce significant drag... as much as _____ percent of the boat's total resistance... a folding prop helps eliminate this problem.

PHOTO: COURTESY OF SEA TOW, BY CAPT. DUKE OVERSTREET, CORTEZ, FL

In any situation where towing assistance is required... **How can you avoid or limit the extent of a salvage claim?**

PHOTO: COURTESY OF THE U.S. COAST GUARD

When underway at night, avoid using white lights (they will temporarily impair your "night vision"). Recovery from exposure to a bright light may take up to _____ minutes.

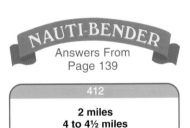

NAUTI-BENDER
Answers From
Page 139

412

2 miles
4 to 4½ miles

413

true wind from astern
vessel's speed

414

0.0 to 0.05 miles
(approximately 100 yards)

PHOTO: BY JOHN SNYDER, NORTH CONWAY, NH

The inward curving of the topsides above the waterline is referred to as a "_____" design.

Most boats, regardless of size, have a series of "_____ holes" cut or built into the transverse members which allow bilge water to drain to the lowest point.

NAUTI-BENDER
Answers From Page 140

415

Water Displacement... 40th try.

416

False: they must be displayed in only one place
(usually the transom)

417

line cutters
(But don't let the lobstermen see them!)

"_____" construction: a method of boat building in which the side planks are butt together flush and the seams caulked to make a smooth finish.

424

A powerful small boat that pushes or pulls an unpowered passenger schooner is called a "_____ boat".

425

PHOTO: BY JOHN SNYDER, NORTH CONWAY, NH

The mark, usually inside the compass bowl, from which one reads the course or steers, is referred to as the "_____ _____".

426

An easily-stowed boarding ladder, which has wooden rungs and is usually supported by rope on either side is referred to as a "_____ *Ladder*".

NAUTI-BENDER
Answers From Page 141

418

20 percent

419

Clearly establish the terms in ADVANCE in writing, on tape, or witnessed.

420

30 minutes

PHOTO: COURTESY OF HUNTER YACHTS

To improve sailing performance while beating, the Skipper should **ease** or **tighten** the sheet?

PHOTO: COURTESY OF SABRE YACHTS

Assuming the sails are set and trimmed properly, as the vessel luffs from beam-reach to close-hauled, the apparent wind will move **forward** or **aft**.

NAUTI-BENDER
Answers From Page 142

421

tumblehome design

422

limber holes (These should be checked and cleaned on a regular basis if possible.)

423

Carvel

PHOTO: COURTESY OF CATALINA YACHTS, BY TOM VIOLAND

To maintain forward speed when maneuvering from *close reach* to a *broad reach*, you should: **ease** or **haul in** the sheets and shift weight **inboard** or **outboard**.

When sailing close-hauled, if you ease the sheets to a point just prior to luffing, you will sail **faster** or **slower**?

Keeping a deep pocket in a sail improves performance in **light** or **heavy air**, particularly while running or reaching.

You're sailing on a close-reach when a gust of wind suddenly heels the boat hard over. To reduce the heeling while maintaining speed, you should ease the main and bear more **into** or **away** from the wind.

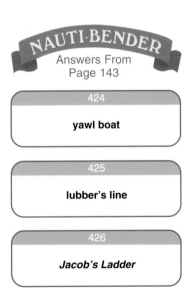

NAUTI-BENDER

Answers From
Page 143

424

yawl boat

425

lubber's line

426

Jacob's Ladder

Removing which element of the "fire triangle": **fuel**, **heat**, or **oxygen** will extinguish a fire?

Electrical fires should be extinguished by: first _____ the power to the affected unit; then dousing with **water**; **Type B**; or **Type C** extinguisher.

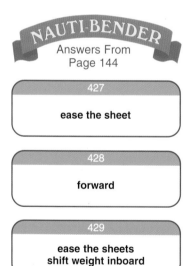

NAUTI-BENDER
Answers From
Page 144

427

ease the sheet

428

forward

429

**ease the sheets
shift weight inboard**

The main advantage of using an alcohol cooking stove is... if a fire should erupt, it can be put out with _____.

PHOTO: COURTESY OF THE U.S. COAST GUARD

You discover a cracked fuel line and fuel is being sprayed on the hot engine. What should you do first: (A) **declare a Mayday**, (B) **stand by with a fire extinguisher**, or (C) **shut off the fuel supply**?

PHOTO: COURTESY OF THE U.S. COAST GUARD

Rule-of-Thumb: The best time to fight an onboard fire is when it _____ starts or is a small fire... please install smoke detectors and fire extinguishers and be familiar with fire-fighting procedures.

Typical marine fire extinguishers (type B-1) have a discharge time of: **8 to 20 seconds**; **30 to 60 seconds**; or **1 to 2 minutes**. When it's discharged and the fire is still raging... what do you do then?

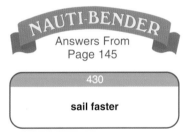

NAUTI-BENDER
Answers From
Page 145

430
sail faster

431
light air

432
bear away from the wind

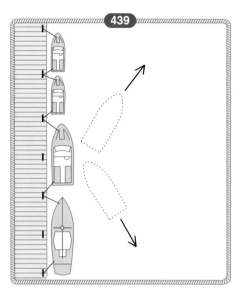

In general, is it better to motor off a dock **bow** or **stern** first?

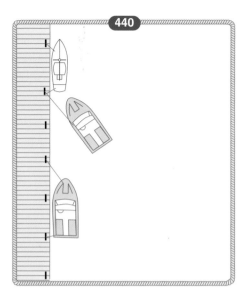

A _____ _____ line can be utilized to get into a tight slip with the engine slow _____ and the rudder hard _____.

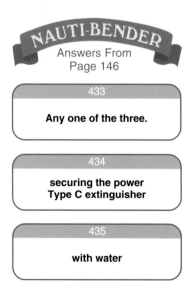

NAUTI-BENDER
Answers From
Page 146

433

Any one of the three.

434

**securing the power
Type C extinguisher**

435

with water

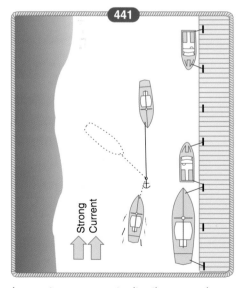

In a strong current situation, as shown above, an "_____ turn" can be useful. Approach as slowly as possible (use reverse if necessary), start the turn, and let the anchor go. As it fetches up, the stern will swing around.

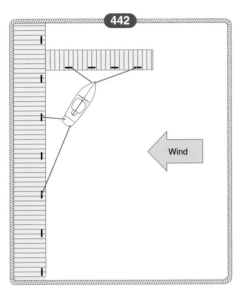

A windward berth may prove uncomfortable for overnight crew. If space permits, moor across a corner with the lines _____ so the boat stays away from the dock.

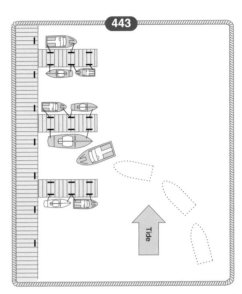

Docking Crisis: While docking in normal fashion, a steering or engine failure occurs... **what action does the Skipper take next**?

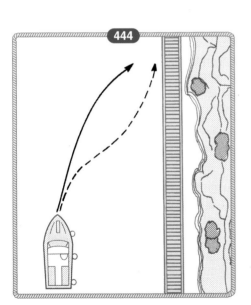

When docking a boat "side-to" with a strong wind off the dock... should the approaching turning angle be **increased** or **decreased**?

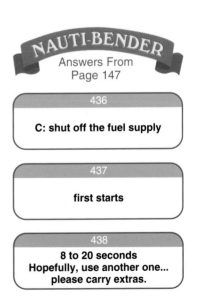

NAUTI-BENDER
Answers From
Page 147

436

C: shut off the fuel supply

437

first starts

438
8 to 20 seconds
Hopefully, use another one...
please carry extras.

445

To make fenders look like new and avoid time-consuming scrubbing, simply wipe them down with a soft rag and some _____.

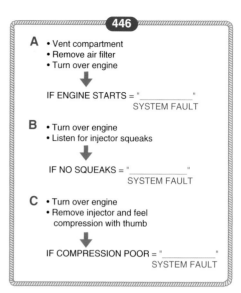

446

A
• Vent compartment
• Remove air filter
• Turn over engine

↓

IF ENGINE STARTS = "_____"
SYSTEM FAULT

B
• Turn over engine
• Listen for injector squeaks

↓

IF NO SQUEAKS = "_____"
SYSTEM FAULT

C
• Turn over engine
• Remove injector and feel compression with thumb

↓

IF COMPRESSION POOR = "_____"
SYSTEM FAULT

If a diesel engine fails to start, three basic systems: "**A**" _____, "**B**" _____, and "**C**" _____ (as described above) should be checked until the fault is isolated.

NAUTI-BENDER
Answers From
Page 148

439
stern first (Takes advantage of the curved bow, plus less draft... no motor at the bow.)

440
**forward spring
slow astern
hard left**

441
anchor turn

447

When changing filters, to prevent your engine(s) from becoming _____ bound and to protect against unnecessary wear... fill the filters with fuel or lube oil prior to installation.

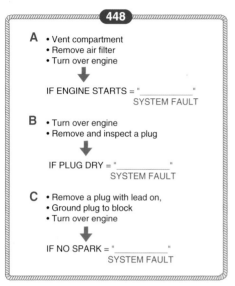

448

A
- Vent compartment
- Remove air filter
- Turn over engine

↓

IF ENGINE STARTS = "_____"
SYSTEM FAULT

B
- Turn over engine
- Remove and inspect a plug

↓

IF PLUG DRY = "_____"
SYSTEM FAULT

C
- Remove a plug with lead on,
- Ground plug to block
- Turn over engine

↓

IF NO SPARK = "_____"
SYSTEM FAULT

If a gasoline engine fails to start, three basic systems: "**A**" _____; "**B**"_____; and "**C**" _____ (as described above) should be checked until the problem is isolated.

449

PHOTO: COURTESY OF ALDEN YACHTS

"_____" is the main reason halyards and sheets part, usually caused by unfair leads.

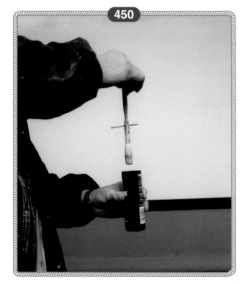

450

Have your paint brushes become solidified with the bristles stuck together? Before discarding, try dipping the brush in hot _____ for a few minutes and then rinse in soapy water.

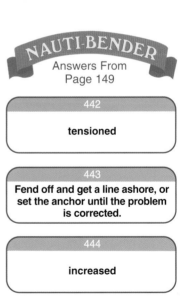

NAUTI-BENDER
Answers From
Page 149

442

tensioned

443

Fend off and get a line ashore, or set the anchor until the problem is corrected.

444

increased

The effective range of a 15 lb. CO_2 extinguisher is: **2 to 4 feet**; **3 to 8 feet**; or **9 to 12 feet**; and it should be sprayed at the **top** or the **base** of the flames.

Most survivors of a crew-overboard situation credit their good fortune to **staying calm** and **keeping a positive mental attitude** while conserving personal _____, maximizing _____, and conserving body _____.

NAUTI-BENDER
Answers From
Page 150

445

Acetone
(Use in a well ventilated area.)

446

A: air
B: fuel
C: ignition

447

air bound

It's a beautiful, bright sunny day. Unfortunately, while taking in the sites, you hit a submerged log and have holed the boat. To signal nearby boats, should you **launch an aerial flare** or **use a smoke flare**?

In an emergency, diesel engines can be run completely underwater, provided the **fuel supply**, **battery**, or **air intake** is above water.

High in the sky off your starboard bow, you observe a green flare hanging from a parachute, indicating a submarine is: (A) **surfacing**; (B) **in distress**; or (C) **conducting a torpedo test**.

If standard PFDs have from 15.5 to 22 pounds of buoyancy... **how can they support a 200-pound person in the water**?

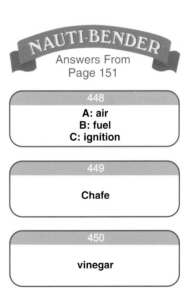

NAUTI-BENDER
Answers From
Page 151

448
A: air **B: fuel** **C: ignition**

449
Chafe

450
vinegar

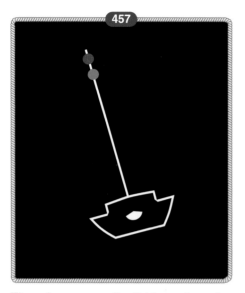

457

The above vessel's light configuration would indicate that she is a _____.

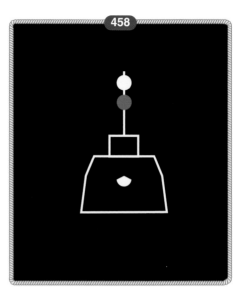

458

The above vessel's light configuration would indicate she is a _____ _____.

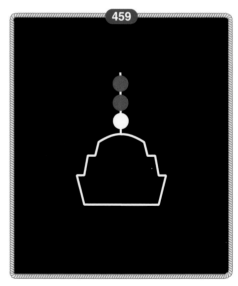

459

The above vessel's light configuration would indicate that she is _____.

What does the above vessel's light configuration (international waters) indicate to the mariner?

The above vessel's light configuration would indicate she is _____ _____.

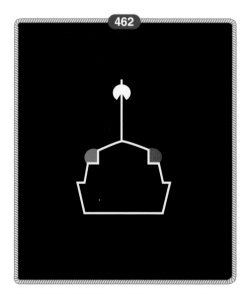

Navigational lights must be displayed in conditions of reduced visibility (fog, rain, or snow) and between _____ and _____.

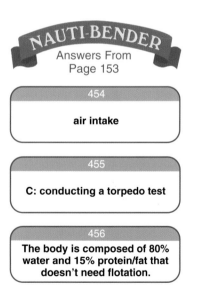

NAUTI-BENDER

Answers From Page 153

454

air intake

455

C: conducting a torpedo test

456

The body is composed of 80% water and 15% protein/fat that doesn't need flotation.

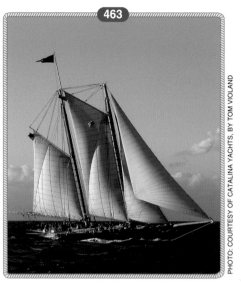

463

PHOTO: COURTESY OF CATALINA YACHTS, BY TOM VIOLAND

"It is undeniable that the beauty of a yacht depends more on her _____ than on any other line on the boat."

-- *Douglas Phillips-Birt*

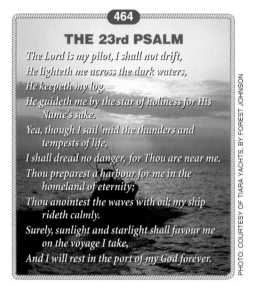

464

THE 23rd PSALM

The Lord is my pilot, I shall not drift,
He lighteth me across the dark waters,
He keepeth my log.
He guideth me by the star of holiness for His
*   Name's sake.*
Yea, though I sail 'mid the thunders and
*   tempests of life,*
I shall dread no danger, for Thou are near me.
Thou preparest a harbour for me in the
*   homeland of eternity;*
Thou anointest the waves with oil; my ship
*   rideth calmly.*
Surely, sunlight and starlight shall favour me
*   on the voyage I take,*
And I will rest in the port of my God forever.

PHOTO: COURTESY OF TIARA YACHTS, BY FOREST JOHNSON

The _____ version of the 23rd psalm.

NAUTI-BENDER
Answers From Page 154

457

sailboat
("red over green...
sailing machine")

458

Pilot boat
"white over red – pilot ahead"

459

aground

465

"The beautiful yacht may not be the driest, most comfortable, or even the fastest; she may even be as lacking in the principal virtues as the most beautiful woman often is, but still she will always be the most desirable. Her faults will be overlooked, and it will be a pleasure to correct her shortcomings."

"Make her _____!" ... says L. Francis Herreshoff.

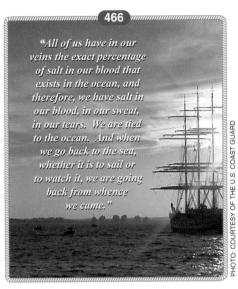

466

"All of us have in our veins the exact percentage of salt in our blood that exists in the ocean, and therefore, we have salt in our blood, in our sweat, in our tears. We are tied to the ocean. And when we go back to the sea, whether it is to sail or to watch it, we are going back from whence we came."

PHOTO: COURTESY OF THE U.S. COAST GUARD

The above is a direct quote from: **Mark Twain**; **John F. Kennedy**; or **Oliver Wendell Holmes**.

467

GRAPHIC BY GINNY HOWE

"For the first time, not on paper and or in dreams, I had a little ship alone in my hands in a night of velvet dark below and stars above, pushing steadily along into unknown waters. I was extremely _____!"

--Arthur Ransome

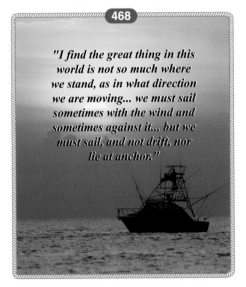

468

"I find the great thing in this world is not so much where we stand, as in what direction we are moving... we must sail sometimes with the wind and sometimes against it... but we must sail, and not drift, nor lie at anchor."

Words of wisdom from: **Joshua Slocum**; **Mark Twain**; or **Oliver Wendell Holmes**?

NAUTI-BENDER
Answers From
Page 155

460

A vessel constrained by draft.

461

towing astern
(tow less than 200M)

462

sunset and sunrise

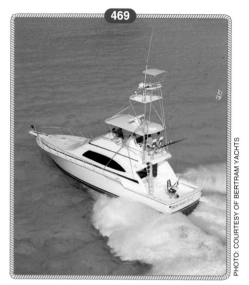

PHOTO: COURTESY OF BERTRAM YACHTS

PHOTO: COURTESY OF TIARA YACHTS

After being underway for a couple of hours, your engine starts running very hot. Which of the following is not the problem: (A) **raw-water intake is clogged**; (B) **thermostat is stuck shut**; or (C) **raw-water impeller has failed**.

Underway on twin engines, what actions will quickly turn the boat to starboard: (A) **reverse port engine, hard right rudder**; (B) **reverse starboard engine, rudder amidships**; or (C) **reverse starboard engine, hard right rudder**?

NAUTI-BENDER
Answers From
Page 156

463
sheer

464
The Mariner's version

465
beautiful

PHOTO: COURTESY OF SEA TOW

If the towline is kept taut, while towing in rough seas, undue stress will be put on both vessels' deck hardware. One method to reduce this stress is to maintain a "_____", to keep the towline under water at all times.

While *gunkholing*, your vessel gently runs aground. You back off the sandbar slowly, then the bilge alarm sounds (the stuffing box is leaking badly)... **what should you do next**?

When a large ship proceeds up a relatively confined and shallow waterway (in relationship to the ship's draft), a _____ effect is created which can violently rock the boats moored along its path.

NAUTI·BENDER
Answers From
Page 157

466

John F. Kennedy

467

happy

468

Oliver Wendell Holmes

Approaching a channel inlet on a flood tide, you observe an onshore wind and five-foot rollers at the mouth. You should ride: (A) **on the back of**; (B) **in front of**; or (C) **on the crest of** a roller and take it in.

A "_____" light remains illuminated at all times when in use.

"Equal _____ lights" are illuminated for periods of time equal to the time of darkness.

NAUTI-BENDER
Answers From Page 158

469
B: This problem would have occurred shortly after starting the engine.

470
C: reverse starboard engine, hard right rudder

471
catenary
(curve of the towline between the tug and tow)

"_____" lights flash at intervals, with the period of light being longer than the period of darkness.

A "_____ flashing" light flashes twice or more times in regular intervals.

"_____" lights show a single flash at regular intervals, with the period of light always being shorter than the period of darkness. This light will flash less than **30**, **50**, or **80** times per minute.

"_____ _____ _____" are white lights only. The groups have different combinations of flashes, e.g., (1 + 3) or one flash and then three flashes of light.

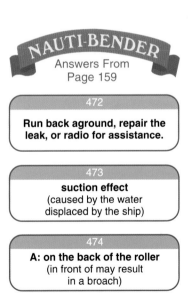

NAUTI-BENDER
Answers From Page 159

472

Run back aground, repair the leak, or radio for assistance.

473

suction effect
(caused by the water displaced by the ship)

474

A: on the back of the roller
(in front of may result in a broach)

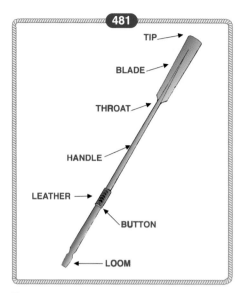

For strength and long life, the best hard-wood oars are made of **spruce**, **ash**, **cedar**, **fir**, or **maple** wood. Which of the descriptors shown in the above graphic have been transposed?

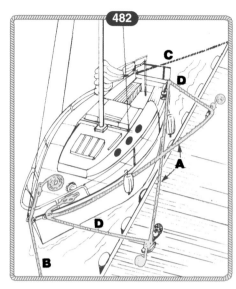

Name the lines in the graphic shown above.

NAUTI-BENDER

Answers From
Page 160

475
fixed

476
Equal interval lights

477
Occulting lights

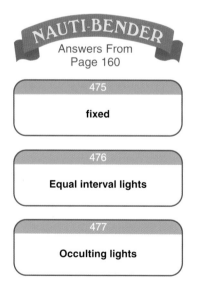

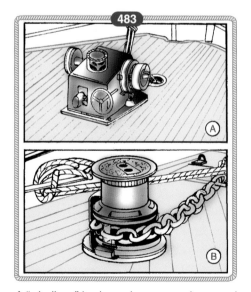

A "windlass" is shown in _____ above and a "capstan" is shown in _____ above.

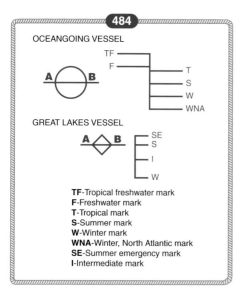

OCEANGOING VESSEL

GREAT LAKES VESSEL

TF-Tropical freshwater mark
F-Freshwater mark
T-Tropical mark
S-Summer mark
W-Winter mark
WNA-Winter, North Atlantic mark
SE-Summer emergency mark
I-Intermediate mark

484

The "_____", or load-line mark, is painted (midships on both sides of merchant vessels) to indicate safe levels of submergence.

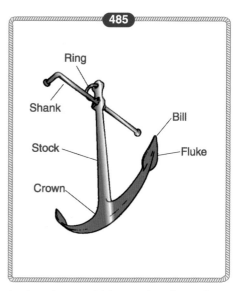

485

In the above, which two descriptors have been transposed?

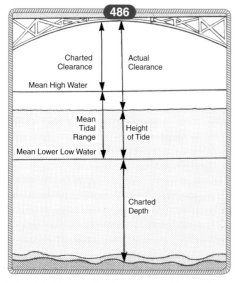

486

The Righteous Brothers not withstanding, there is no such thing as an "ebb tide"...
True or **False**?

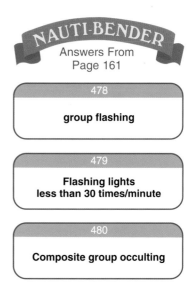

NAUTI-BENDER
Answers From
Page 161

478

group flashing

479

**Flashing lights
less than 30 times/minute**

480

Composite group occulting

In rough anchorages, susceptible to wakes or waves, rubber "_____" or shock absorbers can help eliminate dock line surges which can be potentially harmful to cleats, chocks, etc.

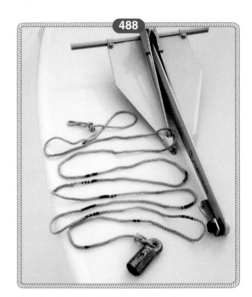

Basic Anchor Watch: If you're unsure of the holding ground, lower a lead line (leave plenty of slack) and secure it to the boat. If the line becomes **taut** or **loose**, the anchor may be dragging.

NAUTI-BENDER
Answers From Page 162

481

ash wood
loom should be *handle*
and vice versa

482

**A: spring; B: bow
C: stern; D: breast**

483

A: windlass (horizontal axis)
B: capstan (vertical axis)

While anchored for lunch at your favorite cove, you check the tension of the anchor rode and it appears to be vibrating... **what does this indicate**?

If your boat has a bow eye, the mooring pendants' lengths should be rigged such that the line going to the _____ takes the stress and the line(s) going to the deck _____ act as a backup.

Some Skippers paint *length* indicators on their anchor *rode* (line or chain). This aid is helpful in laying out enough *rode* to ensure a proper "_____".

Give two reasons why it is not desirable to rig pendants to a mooring ball eye as shown above.

NAUTI-BENDER
Answers From
Page 163

484
Plimsoll mark

485
"Shank" has been transposed with "Stock" and vice versa.

486
True ("Tide" is vertical movement, "current" is horizontal flow, thus "ebb current".)

Red daymarks have a triangular shape since the silhouette resembles the top of a _____ buoy and are _____ numbered.

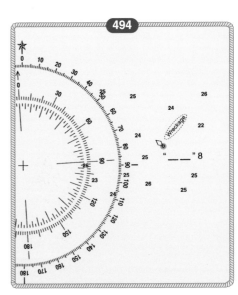

What color are wreck buoys? On charts wreck buoys are in the regular number sequence preceded by what designation?

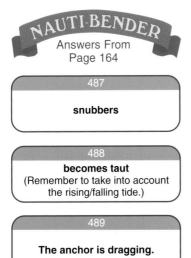

NAUTI-BENDER
Answers From
Page 164

487
snubbers

488
becomes taut
(Remember to take into account the rising/falling tide.)

489
The anchor is dragging.

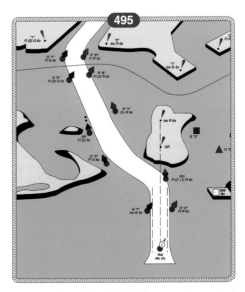

Which of the following indicates a buoy that should be passed to port when entering from seaward: (A) **white light**; (B) **group flashing characteristic**; (C) **a nun buoy**; or (D) **an odd numbered buoy**?

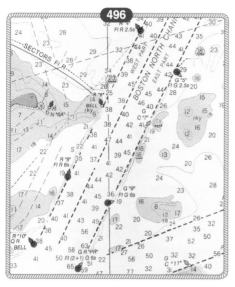

The number sequence on buoys **increases** or **decreases** from seaward.

Green daymarks have a square shape since the silhouette resembles the top of a _____ buoy and are _____ numbered; plus... some of them are great for nesting.

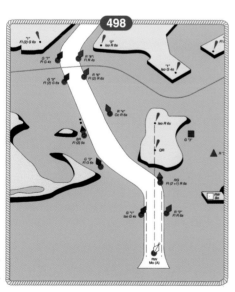

Which buoys are lettered vs. numbered: **green can buoys**; **red nun buoys**; **preferred channel buoys**; and/or **isolated danger buoys**?

Answers From
Page 165

490
bow eye (strongest attachment point takes the load) **deck cleat** (longer, backup)

491
proper *scope*

492
1. **weaker attachment point**
2. **The chain can get twisted and fouled.**

Chain size is referred to by the _____ of any part of the individual links, measured in increments of inches (for example: 3/16", 1/4", 5/16", etc.).

Bow Line

Even the most experienced seamen have mishaps. This potentially embarrassing and dangerous situation was averted by the standard practice of never having a bow line that is longer than the boat's _____ _____.

NAUTI-BENDER
Answers From Page 166

493
nun buoy **even** (like nun buoys)

494
red or green **WR**

495
D: an odd numbered buoy

Many yachtsmen keep excess mooring lines looking neat on the deck by laying out the line in tight successive circles with the "bitter end" in the center... this practice is referred to as "_____".

"One hand for the _____ and one hand for
_____". Rigging lines/fenders on narrow
cat walks can be a somewhat dangerous
operation even in calm seas. Installing
some simple hand holds in strategic locations can lessen the problem.

PHOTO: BY JOHN SNYDER, NORTH CONWAY, NH

Chain "links" are either open or studded.
Stud link chain has a cross member, usually the same diameter as the links, added to
the center of the link. Studding prevents
the chain from _____ and increases its
strength by _____%.

When moored or anchored, a vessel's
mooring lines should be protected with
some type of "_____ _____".

NAUTI-BENDER
Answers From
Page 167

496

increases

497

can
odd numbered like can buoys

498

preferred channel
and isolated danger buoys

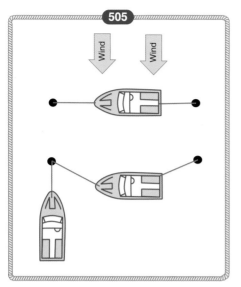

If tied up between moorings or piles side-to a gale, the strain on the boat and mooring lines can be reduced by slacking off both lines (longer lines equal less stress); or if leeway exists, let go the _____ line and lie head-into the wind.

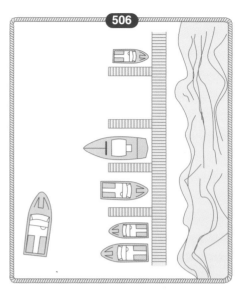

Your vessel has a single right-handed propeller. If you were docking bow-in, would it be easier **port** or **starboard side-to**?

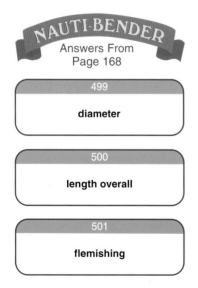

NAUTI-BENDER
Answers From Page 168

499
diameter

500
length overall

501
flemishing

If it's necessary to move a boat single-handedly, the above method will keep the _____ pointed out and keep her from rubbing along the _____.

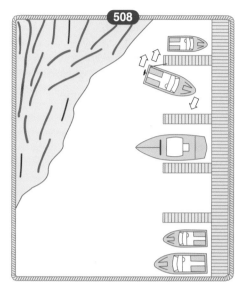

Departing with little room astern can be made easy by utilizing a short back spring with the engine(s) _____ slow and the rudder **right**, **left**, or **amidships**.

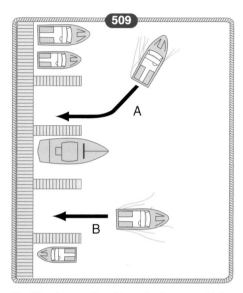

Backing into a slip with a single screw (right-handed propeller) with no wind or current, which of the approaches shown would be better: "**A**" or "**B**"?

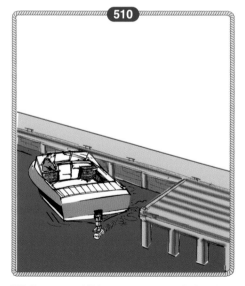

While some I/O's may steer a little sluggishly at _____ speeds, they are great for _____ your way out of a tight slip (the hull will "follow" the prop).

Lavatory facilities on early naval vessels were typically located in the foremost part of the ship, thus the modern day term "the _____".

Baggy wrinkle is a nautical term for: **an incorrectly trimmed sail; an old, badly wrinkled nautical char**t; or **a device to prevent sail chafe**.

NAUTI-BENDER
Answers From
Page 170

505

stern line

506

port side-to
(Boat will tend to back to port.)

507

bow
dock

"Dock" in the strictest meaning of the term, refers to the structure (pier, wharf, quay, etc.) which a boat ties up to – **True** or **False**?

The metal fitting on the inboard end of a boom, which allows movement in all directions is referred to as the: (A) "**lizard**"; (B) "**spider band**"; (C) "**boom swiveler**"; or (D) "**gooseneck**".

When two or more boats are tied side by side while at anchor, at a mooring, or at a dock, it is referred to as "_____".

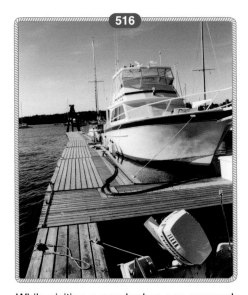

While visiting a new harbor, you approach a salty-looking local and ask permission to tie up at the pier. The old salt replies: "you mean this 'wharf'?" Is there a difference between a pier and a wharf?

NAUTI-BENDER
Answers From
Page 171

508
engine(s) back slow amidships

509
A
(A right-handed prop will make the boat back toward the left.)

510
slow speeds pulling

517

PHOTO: COURTESY OF HATTERAS YACHTS

Set the Alarm: The alarm depth that you select on the depth sounder depends on the danger point's depth and the _____ that you are travelling.

518

PHOTO: COURTESY OF SEA TOW, BY CAPT. DUKE OVERSTREET, CORTEZ.

If you were planning to tow alongside and you had to maneuver a series of four sharp right-hand turns... which side of the disabled vessel (or seaplane) would you tie up to: **port** or **starboard**?

NAUTI-BENDER
Answers From
Page 172

511

the head

512

a device to prevent sail chafe
(always baggy wrinkle – never used in the plural)

513

False – Refers to the water where the boat sits... hence "dry dock".

519

For a smoother ride in rough waters, maneuver in behind a larger vessel and stay within its wake to the right or left of the _____ _____.

Wind will have the most effect on a vessel when she is: **backing down**; **going slow ahead**; **going full ahead**; or **turning**.

When the wind *breezes up*, the hardest course to sail is _____, because there is always the possibility of an accidental jibe or broach.

Before attempting a night passage, ensure that the skipper is experienced, and the crew can perform all necessary shipboard routines in the _____.

NAUTI-BENDER
Answers From
Page 173

514

D: gooseneck

515

rafting

516

Yes (A pier extends perpendicularly into the water. A wharf is parallel to the shore.)

Burgee Flag Etiquette: Modern sailing vessels fly burgees from a lanyard under the **starboard** or **port** spreader (older vessels from the mast head). Power vessels fly them off a short staff on the **bow** or **stern**.

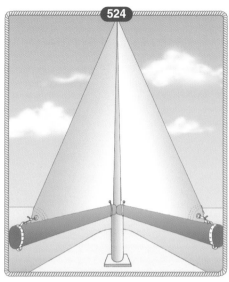

Right-of-Way Rule of Thumb: When you are sailing and meet another sailing vessel head to head, if **your** boom is on the starboard – you should _____ _____; if **your** boom is on the port – you should _____ _____.

NAUTI-BENDER
Answers From
Page 174

517
speed (Factor in a 30-second safety margin. A boat going 30 kts will travel 50 ft/sec.)

518
port side (The tug will turn more easily toward the tow than away from it.)

519
prop wash

The U.S. Coast Guard Navigation Rules are the same for both inland and international waterways – **True** or **False**?

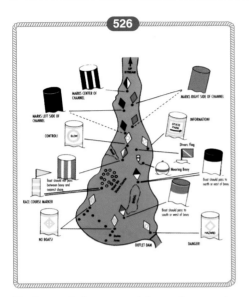

You're exploring a new lake and encounter a line of white buoys with yellow lettering that read "No Bodily Contact"... what does this mean to the Mariner?

Anchoring Etiquette: First _____, first _____; should two vessels swing together, the responsibility lies with the vessel that anchored _____.

You're heading out on an unfamiliar, 50-square mile lake for a weekend of fishing and water-skiing... at what point can you bring the boat up on plane?

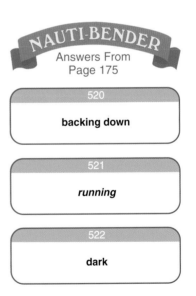

NAUTI-BENDER
Answers From
Page 175

520

backing down

521

running

522

dark

529

You are getting black smudge marks on your boat from the trailer rollers. How can this problem be eliminated?

530

RAMP MANIA

1. **Not using parking brake or tire chock.**
2. **Inability to back the trailer.**
3. **Submerging the trailer too much or too little.**
4. **Not using a coupler-locking pin.**
5. **Starting the engine without a water source.**
6. **Removing the bow eye strap prematurely.**
7. **Blocking ramp an inordinate amount of time.**

Any of the above can produce frustrating, embarrassing, and expensive consequences, that can be avoided with a little practice, planning, and courtesy. Which of the most common launching mistakes has been omitted?

NAUTI-BENDER
Answers From
Page 176

523

**starboard
bow**

524

**starboard – give way
port – stand on**

525

False
(The rules are different... see
"Navigation Rules M16672.2B".)

531

BOAT RETRIEVAL

1. **Back down the trailer until the tops of the fenders are awash.**
2. **Maneuver the boat to the trailer slowly, and line up with the center of the trailer.**
3. **Power up on the trailer or winch it on.**
4. **Connect the winch line hook to the bow eye.**
5. **Raise the motor.**
6. **Pull the boat/trailer off the ramp.**
7. **Follow the pre-trailering procedure.**

It's the end of a busy day at the ramp, everybody is anxious to recover and get home... they are all watching every move you make. What is the most significant factor in maneuvering the boat perfectly onto the trailer on the first try?

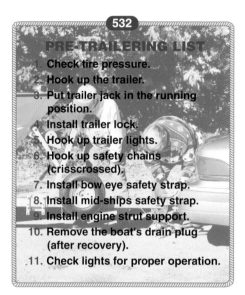

532

PRE-TRAILERING LIST

1. Check tire pressure.
2. Hook up the trailer.
3. Put trailer jack in the running position.
4. Install trailer lock.
5. Hook up trailer lights.
6. Hook up safety chains (crisscrossed).
7. Install bow eye safety strap.
8. Install mid-ships safety strap.
9. Install engine strut support.
10. Remove the boat's drain plug (after recovery).
11. Check lights for proper operation.

What important step has been omitted from the above list?

533

A

B

Which of the bow eye tie-up configurations shown in "**A**" or "**B**" above offers the safest trailering approach... and why?

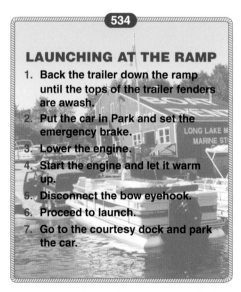

534

LAUNCHING AT THE RAMP

1. Back the trailer down the ramp until the tops of the trailer fenders are awash.
2. Put the car in Park and set the emergency brake.
3. Lower the engine.
4. Start the engine and let it warm up.
5. Disconnect the bow eyehook.
6. Proceed to launch.
7. Go to the courtesy dock and park the car.

Which of the above steps are dependent on the type of boat/trailer you have?

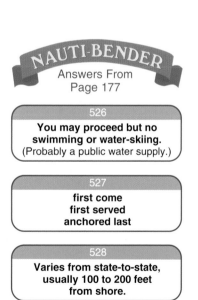

NAUTI-BENDER
Answers From
Page 177

526
You may proceed but no swimming or water-skiing.
(Probably a public water supply.)

527
first come
first served
anchored last

528
Varies from state-to-state, usually 100 to 200 feet from shore.

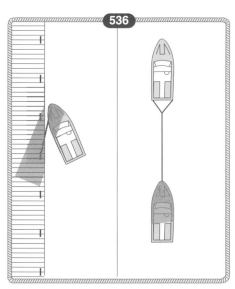

Diesel oil, grease, or gasoline fires should be extinguished: **by dousing with water**; **with a Type B extinguisher**; or **with a Type C extinguisher**.

The _____ of nylon line under load creates danger zones which should be avoided.

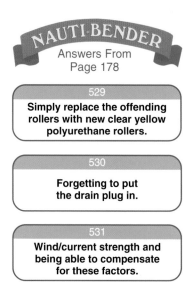

NAUTI-BENDER
Answers From
Page 178

529
Simply replace the offending rollers with new clear yellow polyurethane rollers.

530
Forgetting to put the drain plug in.

531
Wind/current strength and being able to compensate for these factors.

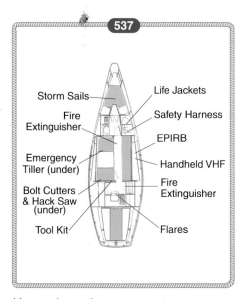

It's good practice to generate an _____ _____ Plan that is prominently displayed for crew and passengers in the event the skipper should fall overboard or otherwise become disabled.

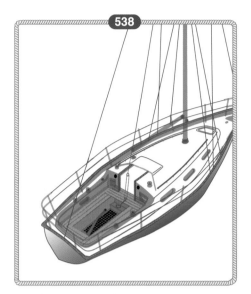

A safety harness is only as good as its attachment point. Life lines, sheets, stanchions, and pulpits are examples of **good** or **poor** attachment points.

PHOTO: COURTESY U.S. COAST GUARD

Crew Overboard: Normally, other crew members **should** or **should not** jump into the water to assist. If necessary, the rescuer should wear a PFD and be tethered to the boat with a strong line.

⚠ **DANGER** ⚠
Exposed Propeller Blades

Before swimming off a boat or recovering a waterskier, **always** stop the engine and put it in _____ to prevent any further prop movement.

NAUTI-BENDER
Answers From
Page 179

532
Ensure that the boat is loaded with all the proper safety equipment.

533
B: Given the right roadway bump, "A" may allow the boat to bounce out of the roller.

534
1: You might not have to submerge the fenders or may have to submerge them 4" to 5".

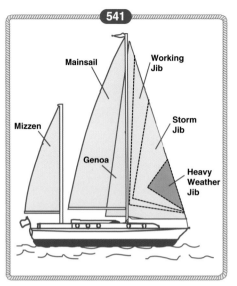

541

Headsails are numbered from the boat's _____ to the _____. Spinnakers are denoted by their _____ _____ and other sails are called by _____.

542

A "_____ _____ rig" has lines rigged on both sides of the mainsail so when lowered, the sail will gather automatically to the boom.

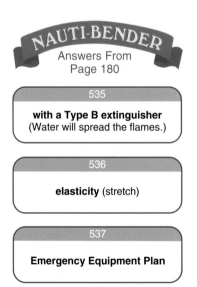

NAUTI·BENDER

Answers From
Page 180

535

with a Type B extinguisher
(Water will spread the flames.)

536

elasticity (stretch)

537

Emergency Equipment Plan

543

In most equipment failure situations, with the materials on board and the sailor's inventiveness, the problem can be temporarily "_____ _____", enabling continued passage.

544

_____ sets of telltales (3 – 12 inches long, depending on the boat's length) should be spaced evenly along the sail's luff and should be bright _____ or _____ for better visibility.

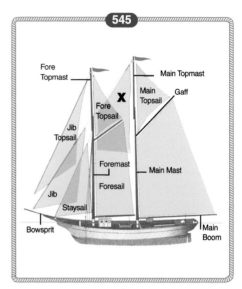

545

Schooner Sail Rig: "**X**" indicated above is referred to as the "_____" sail.

546

A sailor defines wind direction using different words all meaning "toward" or "away": **windward** or "_____", **up** or "_____", **on** or "_____", and **weather** or "_____".

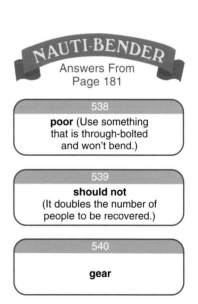

NAUTI-BENDER
Answers From
Page 181

538
poor (Use something that is through-bolted and won't bend.)

539
should not
(It doubles the number of people to be recovered.)

540
gear

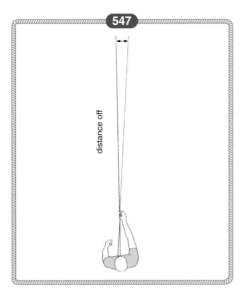

547

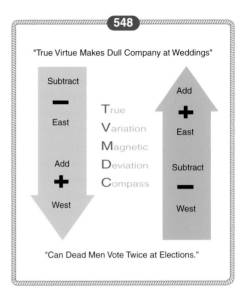

548

"True Virtue Makes Dull Company at Weddings"

Subtract — East

True
Variation
Magnetic
Deviation
Compass

Add + East

Add + West

Subtract — West

"Can Dead Men Vote Twice at Elections."

To Estimate Distance Off: Close your left eye, line up a pencil as shown above, then open your left eye and close the right. Estimate and multiply the distance the pencil has apparently moved (feet, yards, miles) by _____.

You've plotted a course of 60° T. Assuming the variation is at 12° west and deviation is at 5° east... **what compass course should you steer: 53°, 61°, 67°, or 77°?**

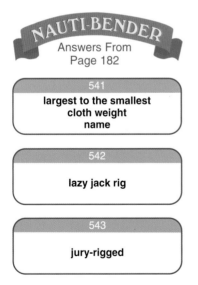

NAUTI-BENDER

Answers From
Page 182

541

largest to the smallest
cloth weight
name

542

lazy jack rig

543

jury-rigged

549

AUGUST

Morning		Boston	Afternoon	
HIGH	4:11	**SUNDAY**	HIGH	4:34
Height	9.8		Height	10.8
LOW	10:18	**14**	LOW	11:00
Height	0.2		Height	-0.1
Sunrise	4:50	FIRST QUARTER	Sunset	6:47
HIGH	5:13	**MONDAY**	HIGH	5:36
Height	9.4		Height	10.7
LOW	11:17	**15**	LOW	———
Height	0.5		Height	———
Sunrise	4:51		Sunset	6:46
HIGH	6:18	**TUESDAY**	HIGH	6:39
Height	9.2		Height	10.7
LOW	12:04	**16**	LOW	12:19
Height	0.0		Height	0.7
Sunrise	4:52		Sunset	6:44
HIGH	7:24	**WEDNESDAY**	HIGH	7:43
Height	9.3		Height	10.7
LOW	1:08	**17**	LOW	1:22
Height	0.0		Height	0.7
Sunrise	4:53		Sunset	6:43
HIGH	8:26	**THURSDAY**	HIGH	8:43
Height	9.4		Height	10.8
LOW	2:09	**18**	LOW	2:23
Height	-0.1		Height	0.5
Sunrise	4:54		Sunset	6:41
HIGH	9:23	**FRIDAY**	HIGH	9:38
Height	9.7		Height	10.9
LOW	3:06	**19**	LOW	3:19
Height	-0.3		Height	0.3
Sunrise	4:55		Sunset	6:40

Tide tables are sometimes shown in "standard time". To correct for daylight savings time, remember: "spring _____ (add one hour), and fall _____ (subtract one hour".

550

SIMPLE WEATHER CODE FOR LOG ENTRIES

- b – blue sky
- c – cloudy
- d – drizzle
- f – fog
- ff – thick fog
- g – gloomy/dark
- h – hail
- l – lightning
- m – mist/haze
- o – overcast
- p – passing showers
- q – squalls
- r – continuous rain
- s – snow
- t – thunder

The above weather codes can be used in various combinations to indicate a complete weather description in the ship's log. For example, **what would the log entry: "glqt" indicate?**

551

Having difficulty identifying individual islands within a cluster? Try scanning across a folded chart with your eye just above your vessel's _____ toward the islands.

552

Speed Table

RPM	East-West Time	Speed (Knots)	East-West Time	Speed (Knots)	Average Speed (Knots)
600	9:22	6.41	9:26	6.36	6.04
1,000	7:28	8.04	7:32	7.96	8.00
1,500	5:36	10.71	5:42	10.53	10.62
2,000	3:28	17.31	3:38	16.51	16.91
2,500	2:48	21.43	2:56	20.45	20.94
3,000	2:24	25.00	2:38	22.78	23.89
3,500	2:04	29.03	2:08	28.13	28.58
4,000	1:50	32.73	1:52	32.40	32.57

$$\text{Speed} = \frac{3600 \text{ seconds}}{\text{Time (seconds)}}$$

$$\text{Average Speed} = \frac{\text{E/W Time} + \text{W/E Time}}{2}$$

If your vessel is not equipped with a speed measuring device, a handy speed table can be calculated using the above formulas and determining the time required to travel a _____ nautical mile course in both directions.

NAUTI-BENDER
Answers From Page 183

544
Three sets
red (starboard) **or** green (port)

545
Fisherman

546
windward or leeward, up or down, on or off, weather or lee

Salvage Claims: Clearly establish the helper's terms before accepting a tow. Also, if possible use **your** or the **would-be rescuer's** towline indicating a "voluntary acceptance of aid".

A ski-boat will have better maneuverability when the tow rope is secured well **forward** or **aft** of the transom.

Answers From
Page 184

547
10

548
67°
("at weddings – add west")
("at elections – add east")

549
spring ahead
fall back

The three main dangers of running before a heavy sea include: "_____"; being "_____"; or being "_____". If these circumstances are likely, it may be time to heave to.

PHOTO: COURTESY OF THE U.S. COAST GUARD

In a crew-overboard situation, in what order would you do the following: (A) **never lose sight of the victim**; (B) **toss a PFD**; (C) **radio in a Mayday**; or (D) **execute a Williamson turn**.

Large ships can _____ the wind from unsuspecting sailors, leaving them without steerage when they need it most!

PHOTO: COURTESY OF THE U.S. COAST GUARD

Before rendering assistance to a disabled vessel, seriously consider the situation. If you feel that you may not be experienced enough or otherwise not equipped for the job – _____ _____ until qualified help arrives.

NAUTI-BENDER
Answers From
Page 185

550

gloomy/dark, lightning, squalls, and thunder

551

position

552

one nautical mile

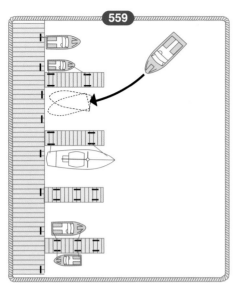

When docking a single-screw vessel (right-hand propeller) starboard side-to, if you back down to stop the boat's forward motion with the rudder amidships... you would expect the bow to turn **towards** or **away** from the dock.

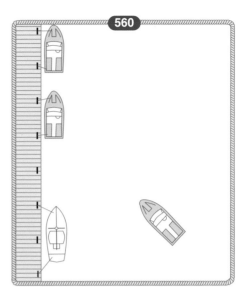

The best conditions to maneuver into a tight slip would be: (A) **with the wind off the dock**; (B) **with the wind onto the dock**; (C) **at slack tide ("tidal stand")**; or (D) **with a cross current**.

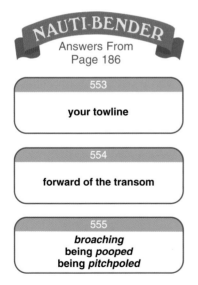

NAUTI-BENDER
Answers From
Page 186

553

your towline

554

forward of the transom

555

broaching
being *pooped*
being *pitchpoled*

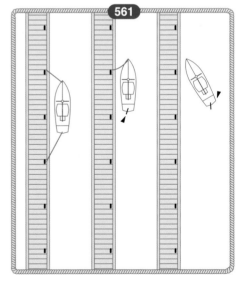

The above unberthing procedure would be proper with the wind coming **onto** or **off** the dock and the tidal current from **ahead** or **astern**.

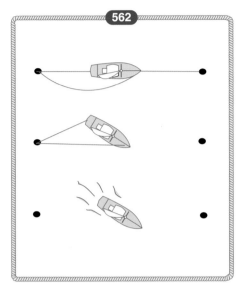

When tied-up between moorings or piles, stern-to the wind, or tidal current, a long bow line can be utilized to "_____" the stern out for easy departure.

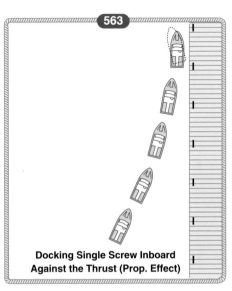

Docking Single Screw Inboard Against the Thrust (Prop. Effect)

Approach normally, except that before you get to the stopping point, apply a short burst of power **forward** or **astern** to get the stern swinging to _____, then apply a short burst **forward** or **astern** to stop.

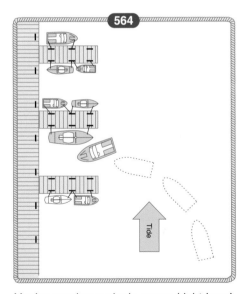

You're running a single-screw (right-handed propeller) vessel, when the stern swings into danger on a turn... what compensating action is required by the Skipper?

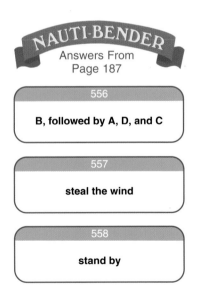

NAUTI-BENDER

Answers From Page 187

556
B, followed by A, D, and C

557
steal the wind

558
stand by

Winter Storage: Boats up to 30' should use two sets of jack stands (legs parallel to the boat's keel). Jack stands are good tie down points for the boat cover – **True** or **False**?

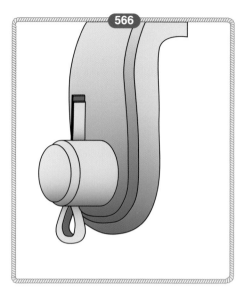

When installing a cotter pin, it should project approximately _____ the fitting's width and be spread at an angle of about _____ degrees, then it should be protected with a couple of wraps of tape.

Answers From
Page 188

559

towards the dock

560

C: at slack tide

561

**wind onto the dock
current from astern**

Barnacles can be easily removed from your prop(s) by bathing them in _____ acid until they are dissolved.

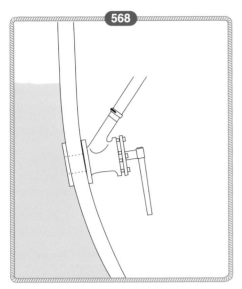

Seacocks should be cycled (opened or closed) on a regular basis to prevent corrosion buildup and they should be lubricated every _____ months or so.

Winter Storage: Should you block the boat so it's sitting **level** or with the **bow slightly up**?

PHOTO: COURTESY OF TIARA YACHTS, BY BOB HARR

Salt water systems on a boat do not need winterizing... **True** or **False**?

Answers From Page 189

562

spring the stern out

563

**forward
starboard
astern**

564

**Hard right rudder
and a quick "burst" of
power forward.**

571

PHOTO: COURTESY OF SEA TOW, BY CAPT. DUKE OVERSTREET, CORTEZ, FL

When towing alongside, your vessel's maneuverability is greatly affected... acceleration will be **enhanced** or **reduced** and stopping ability will be **enhanced** or **reduced**.

572

"Warming up" your engine(s) is accomplished better by **idling at the dock** or **by cruising at about half speed**.

NAUTI-BENDER
Answers From
Page 190

565
False (If the stand settles slightly, the cover could act like a sail and pull it over.)

566
one-half the fitting's width
about 20 degrees

567
muriatic acid
(Wear rubber gloves, goggles, etc.)

573

PHOTO: COURTESY OF BOSTON WHALER BOATS

To safely enjoy waterskiing, it is recommended that a three-member team be used: _____, _____, and _____
_____.

The best method to maneuver to a mooring "pick-up buoy" is **with** or **into** the wind.

PHOTO: COURTESY OF SEA TOW, BY CAPT. DUKE OVERSTREET, CORTEZ, FL

Before accepting a tow, discuss the situation with your would-be rescuers... if they appear _____ or _____, you may be well advised to wait for qualified assistance.

PHOTO: COURTESY OF BOSTON WHALER BOATS

After running for 15 to 20 minutes, your outboard sputters and dies. The cause may be: **fouled plug(s)**; **you're out of gas**; **the fuel tank's vent is shut**; **or any one of the above**.

NAUTI-BENDER
Answers From
Page 191

568

three months

569

level (On an incline, water, dust, and dirt collects in the corners causing stains, rust and rot.)

570

False –
Salt water freezes at
28° Fahrenheit.

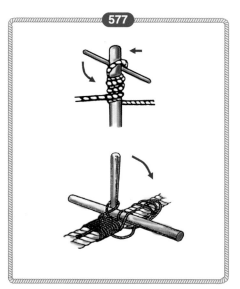

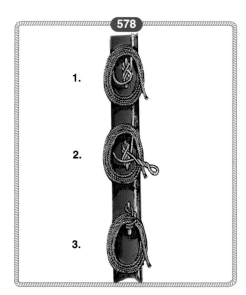

"_____ windlass", a simple leverage method (as shown above) used to draw "seizings" or lashings taut. The same principle can be utilized (like a turnbuckle) in any situation involving rope.

To stow a line so that it remains coiled (assuming it has already been made fast to a cleat) use a halyard _____ as shown above.

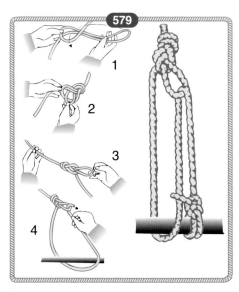

The "_____ hitch" is a handy knot for securing a load such as a dinghy on the foredeck or a small boat on top of a car.

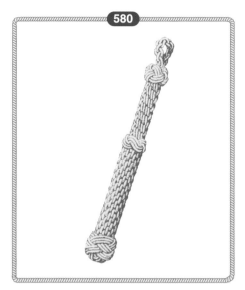

580

Most ropes on board are referred to as "lines"; one exception would be the "_____".

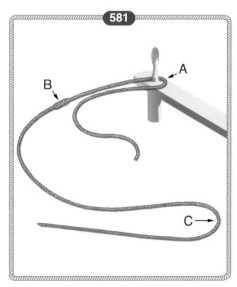

581

Knot Terminology: A: "_____" – a loop around an object. **B**: "_____" – joining two lines together by intertwining the strands. **C**: "_____" – a bend or loop in a line.

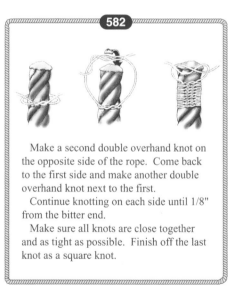

582

Make a second double overhand knot on the opposite side of the rope. Come back to the first side and make another double overhand knot next to the first.

Continue knotting on each side until 1/8" from the bitter end.

Make sure all knots are close together and as tight as possible. Finish off the last knot as a square knot.

"**Whipping**" keeps the end of a line from unraveling and is especially good for frequently/hard-used _____ or _____ lines. The above technique will not come undone if one of the turns is cut or wears away.

NAUTI-BENDER
Answers From
Page 193

574

into the wind

575

unseamanlike or careless

576

any one of the above

583
FIVE EASIEST WAYS TO SINK YOUR BOAT

1. **Not replacing the drain plug:** Use pre-launch check list and keep a spare drain plug in the boat.
2. **Dead battery causing bilge pump failure:** Have the marina keep a good watch.
3. **Hose failure:** Inspect regularly and replace (use double hose clamps).
4. **Being "pooped" or swamped:** Keep sharp lookout for wakes and waves.
5. **Collision with partially submerged flotsam & rocks:** Check up-to-date charts and maintain good lookouts.

Which of the "remedies" given in the above "Five Easiest Ways to Sink Your Boat" is **incorrect**?

584
STORM PROTECTION ON-SHORE

Inside storage is best; however, if you must leave a boat outside:

1. Place boat where trees or other objects won't fall on it.
2. If on trailer: lash the boat securely to the trailer; place trailer frame on blocks; let some air out of and chock tires (to prevent rolling).
3. If possible, remove engine(s).
4. If on jackstands, use extra stands chained together and support with plywood.
5. Fill lighter boats up completely with water to increase stability.
6. Remove antenna and all loose gear.

A hurricane-force storm is predicted for your area. Assuming you have the option of taking your boat out of the water, the above precautionary steps will help protect your vessel... **which suggestion is in error?**

NAUTI-BENDER
Answers From
Page 194

577
Spanish windlass

578
halyard coil

579
trucker's hitch

585
STORM PROTECTION ON THE MOORING

1. Inspect and replace worn mooring gear.
2. Rig a V-shaped "snubber" to the bow cleats and use extra chafing gear.
3. Remove sails or lash down securely.
4. Rig anchor off the bow and stern to hold her into the wind.
5. Remove protruding objects (anchors, etc).
6. Rig fenders all around the boat.

A hurricane-force storm is predicted for your area. Assuming you were going to ride it out on the mooring, the above preventative steps should help protect your vessel. Which of the above given suggestions is in error?

586

STORM PROTECTION AT ANCHOR

1. Look for solid holding ground, such as mud or clay.

2. Anchor by best estimate of wind direction.

3. Use at least three heavy anchors.

4. Use the proper size rode and extra chain.

5. Set anchors with at least 5:1 scope.

6. Have a back-up tie-down rig in case the main cleat(s) pull(s) out.

Your boat is going to ride out a hurricane-force storm at anchor. The above preventative steps should help protect your vessel... **which of the suggestions is in error?**

587

RIDE OUT THE STORM

A. At the marina.

B. On the mooring.

C. Out of the water.

D. Anchored out.

A hurricane-force storm is predicted for your area. List the above options from the safest to the least safe place for your vessel to weather the storm.

588

STORM PROTECTION AT THE MARINA

1. Arrange the bow toward open water or in the most protected direction.

2. Use extra long dockline, doubled or tripled – boat should be in center of spider web.

3. Chafing gear, chafing gear, and more chafing gear.

4. Use plenty of fenders.

5. Ensure batteries will run bilge pumps throughout storm.

6. Keep boat watertight, use tape around windows and hatches.

Your boat is going to ride out a hurricane-force storm at the marina. The above preventative steps should help protect the vessel... **which suggestion is in error?**

NAUTI-BENDER
Answers From
Page 195

580
bellrope (often braided in decorative patterns and terminated in a *Turk's Head*)

581
A: turn B: splice C: bight

582
dock or fender lines

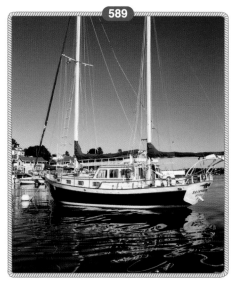

The raised area over the companion way at the aft end of a sailboat's cabin top is sometimes referred to as the "_____ _____".

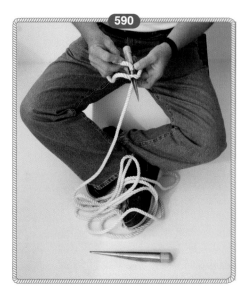

A fid or a "_____ _____" is a smooth, tapered tool used for opening stranded line and for splicing.

NAUTI-BENDER
Answers From
Page 196

583
2. (Don't rely on the marina – install a "smart charger" or use a full canvas cover.)

584
5. (Fill the boat one-third to halfway. Overfilling may cause damage to the boat or trailer.)

585
4. A stern anchor will prevent her from swinging with the wind and could cause capsizing.

A "bumper" is a cushioning device used to protect your boat and a "fender" protects your car... or, is it... a "bumper" protects your car and a "fender" is a cushioning device used to protect your boat?

When a vessel is kept meticulously in every detail, it is said to be kept in "_____ _____".

When a vessel flips over, end for end, bow under first, it is referred to as "_____".

"_____ _____": a narrow strip of paint or tape of contrasting color, applied on the hull between the "bottom" and "topsides" paint, that typically indicates the vessel's natural _____.

NAUTI-BENDER
Answers From
Page 197

586
5.
(Scope should be
at least a 10:1 ratio.)

587
C, B, A, D

588
1. (Bow should be headed toward open water or in the least-protected direction.)

595

PHOTO: COURTESY OF THE U.S. COAST GUARD

At night, in a large, busy harbor – a power-boat Skipper observes a sailboat off the port bow (on a collision course). The sailboat is showing a masthead light, side lights, and a stern light... **what should the Skipper do next**?

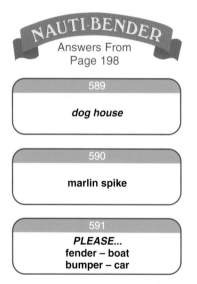

NAUTI-BENDER
Answers From
Page 198

589

dog house

590

marlin spike

591

PLEASE...
fender – boat
bumper – car

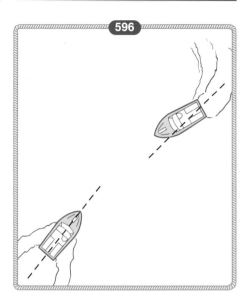

596

In a head-on or crossing situation (in sight visually), to indicate that: "I'm changing course to starboard"... you should sound _____ _____ blast(s).

597

The above vessel's light configuration would indicate that she is restricted in the _____ _____ _____.

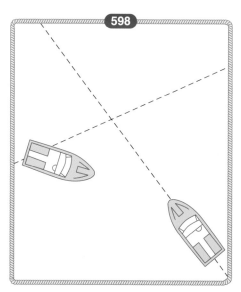

In a crossing situation, proper sound signals should be used. It is customary for the "**stand-on**" or "**give-way**" vessel to signal first.

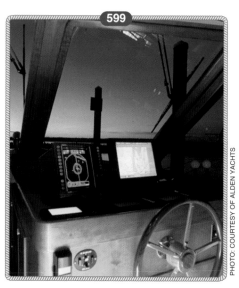

PHOTO: COURTESY OF ALDEN YACHTS

A vessel less than **5**, **7**, or **12 meters** long is **not** required to show an anchor light if anchored in an area not normally navigated.

The above vessel's light configuration would indicate she is _____ .

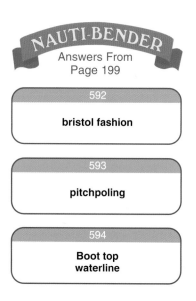

NAUTI-BENDER
Answers From
Page 199

592
bristol fashion

593
pitchpoling

594
**Boot top
waterline**

601

Before rendering assistance to another vessel, bear in mind... your first priority is to ensure that your vessel does not _____ or _____ to the other vessel's problems.

PHOTO: COURTESY OF THE U.S. COAST GUARD

602

A boat will float **lower**, **the same**, or **higher** in fresh water versus saltwater?

NAUTI-BENDER
Answers From
Page 200

595

Maintain course – the sailboat is under power.
(thus the *give way* vessel)

596

one short blast

597

restricted in the ability to maneuver

603

_____ _____ and flapping in the breeze are the major enemies of synthetic sails.

604

Seamanship skills are displayed in many ways. Having fenders rigged while under-way, is an example of poor seamanship... sometimes referred to by old salts as "_____ _____ _____ _____ _____".

605

PHOTO: COURTESY OF THE U.S. COAST GUARD

It is potentially damaging to a powerboat's engine, drive train and propeller to buck a large head sea... **why**?

606

What are most minor petroleum spills caused by?

NAUTI-BENDER
Answers From
Page 201

598

stand-on vessel

599

7 meters
(23 feet)

600

anchored

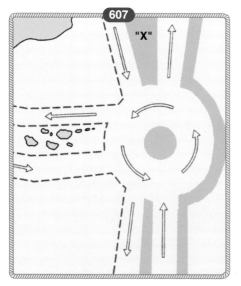

A navigator planning a trip to a busy port studies the associated chart and notes a *traffic separation scheme* (as shown above). What does the area surrounding point "**X**" indicate to the navigator?

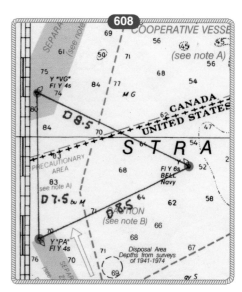

Departing at 0800 hours, what speed is required to complete the following course by 1200 hours: Y "PA" to Y to Y "VG" and then returning to Y "PA". (Hint: use the dead reckoning formula 60D = ST.)

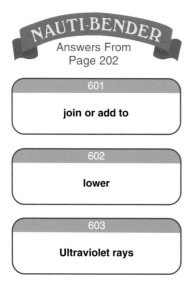

NAUTI-BENDER

Answers From
Page 202

601

join or add to

602

lower

603

Ultraviolet rays

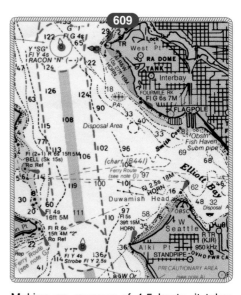

Making an average of 4.5 knots, it takes you 67 minutes to travel from Y "T" to Y "SG". What is the distance between the buoys? (Hint: use the dead reckoning formula 60D = ST).

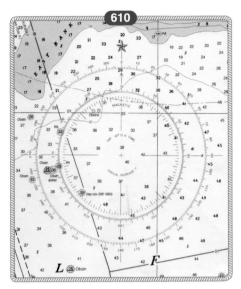

The outer ring of the compass rose indicates _____ direction, the next inner ring indicates _____ direction, and the innermost ring indicates the compass "_____".

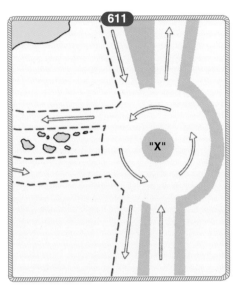

A navigator planning a trip to a busy port studies the associated chart and notices a *traffic separation scheme* (as shown above). What does the area surrounding point "**X**" indicate to the navigator?

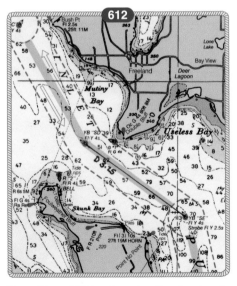

Travelling at 12 knots, using the dead reckoning formula (60D = ST), how long would it take to go from YB "SE" to YB "SD"?

Answers From
Page 203

604

**as having their
laundry hanging out**

605

**The propeller(s) will race when
lifted out of the water...**
putting a strain on the system.

606

human error
(overfilling fuel tanks)

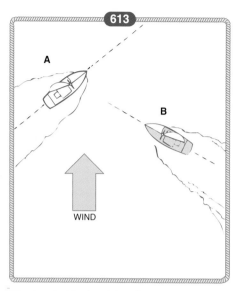

613

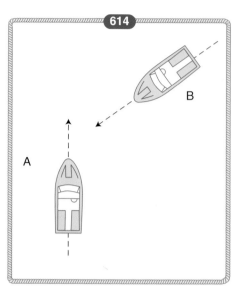

614

The boat with the right-of-way in a head-on or crossing situation is referred to as the _____-_____ vessel. In the above graphic which boat has the right-of-way?

Following the rules of navigation, the *burdened* vessel is the ***stand-on vessel*** or the **give-way** vessel. Which of the vessels shown above is the *give way* vessel?

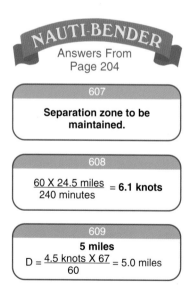

NAUTI-BENDER
Answers From
Page 204

607

Separation zone to be maintained.

608

$$\frac{60 \times 24.5 \text{ miles}}{240 \text{ minutes}} = \textbf{6.1 knots}$$

609

5 miles
$$D = \frac{4.5 \text{ knots} \times 67}{60} = 5.0 \text{ miles}$$

615

If a sailing vessel under sail overtakes a powerboat... which is the "give way" vessel?

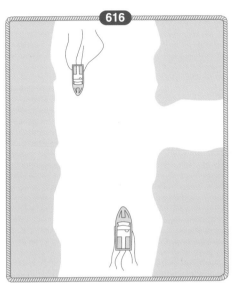

In the above shown "meeting situation" (no current), assuming both vessels are going to turn into the smaller channel at approximately the same time... which is the stand-on vessel?

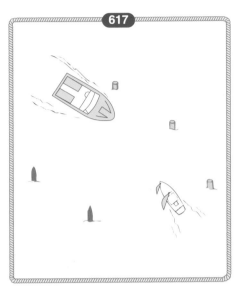

A sailboat **does** or **does not** have to keep clear of a powerboat that cannot navigate outside the channel it's using.

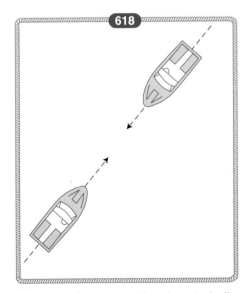

When meeting a vessel head-on, typically, you would pass _____ to _____, unless you make a "two-whistle passing", and then you would pass _____ to _____.

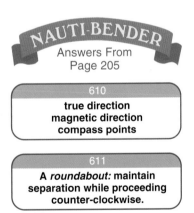

NAUTI-BENDER
Answers From
Page 205

610
true direction
magnetic direction
compass points

611
A *roundabout:* maintain separation while proceeding counter-clockwise.

612
16.25 Minutes
$T = \dfrac{(60 \times 3.25 \text{ miles})}{12 \text{ knots}} = 16.3$

A good skipper will always make sure that his/her crew know what their duties are well before _____ or _____ a berth.

In very tight quarters, even the most experienced captain may have to use the *hand-over-hand* maneuvering technique and "_____" the boat in.

NAUTI-BENDER
Answers From Page 206

613

**stand-on vessel
vessel "A"**

614

***give-way* vessel
vessel A**

615

the sailing vessel

To clear the buoy, when departing from a mooring (light wind/current), you should: (A) **apply a short burst of power, hard-right rudder**; (B) **back a few boat lengths and proceed normally**; or (C) **go half-ahead, hard-right rudder**.

When docking, which line should normally be secured first?

More fenders are typically used by the **more** or **less** experienced Skippers.

Before getting underway, the Skipper should determine the best departure maneuver... **what factors should be taken into consideration**?

NAUTI-BENDER
Answers From
Page 207

616
The rules do not address this situation but imply the vessel turning to the starboard.

617
does

618
**port to port
starboard to starboard**

625

Small-Craft warnings refer to vessels under _____ meters.

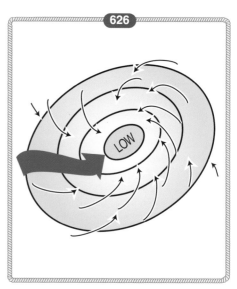

626

A wind that *backs* is changing direction to your **left** or **right** as you face it. This wind shift would indicate an impending weather change: **fair** or **stormy** (northern hemisphere).

NAUTI-BENDER
Answers From
Page 208

619

leaving or approaching
a berth

620

walk or warp the boat in

621

B: back a few boat lengths
and proceed normally.

627

Sea bird observations can be used as weather indicators:
1. Flying out to sea – _____ wind and _____ weather;
2. Flying toward land – _____ wind and _____ weather.

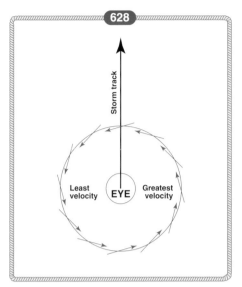

Tropical storms (winds 64 knots plus) advance at speeds up to 25 knots with wind circulating _____ in the northern hemisphere and _____ in the southern hemisphere.

If a vessel becomes "_____" or goes aground on a "spring" high tide, she may have to wait _____ days for the next high tide sufficient to float her off.

Dew in the morning typically indicates a **fair** or a **rainy** day; conversely a dry morning typically indicates a **fair** or a **rainy** day.

NAUTI-BENDER
Answers From
Page 209

622
after bow spring line
(99% of the time)

623
more experienced
(Everyone has a bad landing
occasionally.)

624
**wind's direction/strength;
which lines are under strain;
current's direction/strength**

631

632

"_____" is a term originating from cruise line accommodations offering wealthy passengers cabins on the **p**ort side going **o**ut and the **s**tarboard side coming **h**ome to avoid the sun's heat and glare.

When sail area is reduced during high winds, it is referred to as "_____".

NAUTI-BENDER

Answers From
Page 210

625

20 meters

626

**to your left
stormy weather**

627

1. moderate wind and **fair** weather; **2. strong** wind and **stormy** weather.

633

What is the difference between "pilings" and "dolphins"?

An anchor rode should be previously "_____" to facilitate free running when cast overboard.

PHOTO: COURTESY OF GRAND BANKS YACHTS

Trawler-type boats typically incorporate a small "_____ sail" to dampen the effect of rough seas.

A sailboat with an especially large engine(s) that is typically not very efficient under sail or power, is called a "_____ _____".

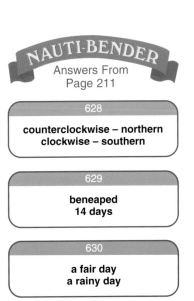

NAUTI-BENDER
Answers From
Page 211

628
**counterclockwise – northern
clockwise – southern**

629
**beneaped
14 days**

630
**a fair day
a rainy day**

Gone Aground: The _____ _____ can be used as a towline to heel the boat over, thus freeing the keel.

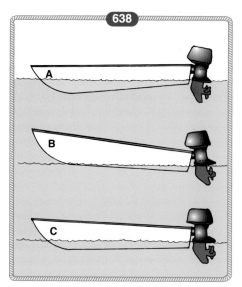

A boat in proper _____ achieves better fuel economy and speed. Which of the boats shown above is in proper _____?

NAUTI-BENDER
Answers From
Page 212

631

POSH
(Port Out Starboard Home)

632

reefing

633

Dolphins are a cluster of three or more pilings usually lashed together with cable.

WIND

Retrieving A Water Skier: Recover the tow line, approach from _____ wind at _____ speed with the skier on the _____ side. When near to the skier shift into neutral, turn-off the engine and then shift into _____.

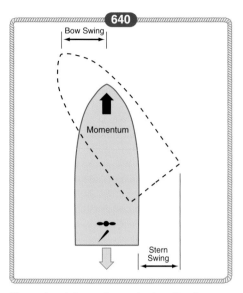

640

Bow Swing

Momentum

Stern Swing

Every boat turns by swinging the **bow** or **stern**.

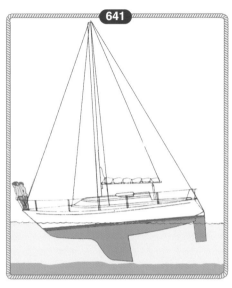

641

When caught aground on a falling tide, you can _____ _____ by heeling the boat over (sails or weight on the extended boom) or by positioning the crew fore or aft.

642

Gone aground (navigable water on both sides)... try keeping a continuous strain on a kedge anchor while another powerboat runs alongside and uses its _____ to float her free.

Some buoys have sound-producing devices including: _____; _____; _____; or _____.

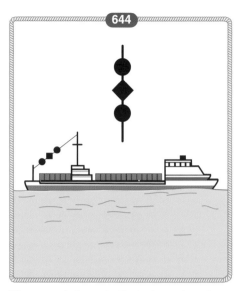

The vessel above is displaying a day shape indicating she is _____ _____ _____.

Answers From Page 214

637

main halyard

638

trim
trim
C

639

down wind; **idle** speed;
driver's side; shift into **gear**
(to stop the propeller)

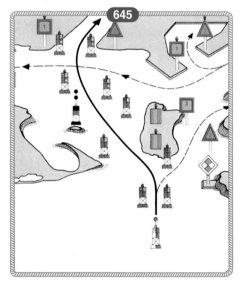

Buoy Sequence: Returning to port from sea: "Red _____ returning".

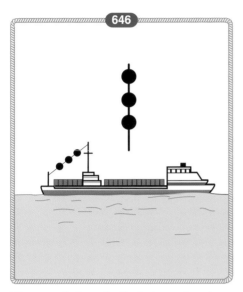

The vessel above is displaying a day shape indicating she is _____ and over _____ meters long.

Cruising southward along the California coast, you encounter a lighted, green buoy which should be kept on the **starboard side**, **port side**, or **either side**... please, not too close – after a big lunch, they are all taking a nice nap.

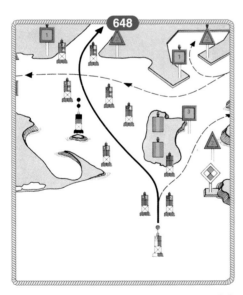

Leaving the harbor, remember "red left _____".

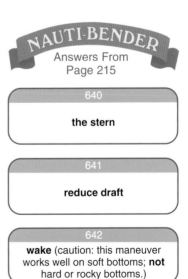

NAUTI-BENDER
Answers From
Page 215

640

the stern

641

reduce draft

642

wake (caution: this maneuver works well on soft bottoms; **not** hard or rocky bottoms.)

In the rare event you should ever have to be rescued by a Coast Guard helicopter, **remember to let the basket hit the water before grabbing it**... the _____ _____ charge could be fatal.

PHOTO: COURTESY OF THE U.S. COAST GUARD

NAUTICAL TRIVIA

1. **People associated with the U.S. Navy or Marines.**
2. **U.S. cities, territories.**
3. **Famous people, old war ships, battles.**
4. **U.S. states.**
5. **Fish, sea life, or famous Americans.**

Nautical Trivia: U.S. Naval ships are named after people, places or things. Match the above categories with the following ship types: (**A**) aircraft carriers; (**B**) battle ships; (**C**) cruisers; (**D**) destroyers; and (**E**) submarines.

NAUTI-BENDER
Answers From
Page 216

643
bells, horns, gongs or whistles

644
restricted in maneuverability

645
right

Water, water everywhere, but not a drop to drink, nor a proper place to perch. The occasional unexpected visit of a winged _____ can break the monotony of a long passage.

652

TO STOP A THIEF!

— Use hitch/wheel locks.

— Secure the boat to the dock with a stainless steel cable and padlock.

— Simply dangle a line overboard (to be caught in the prop).

— Install hidden fuel or electrical power shut offs.

— Remove a spark plug.

— Install LoJack or other security systems.

In the USA, according to Boat/U.S., an average of **500**, **1,000**, or **1,500** boats are stolen each month, costing insurance companies over $100 million a year.

653

Boaters' Advisory: If you see the above vessel on the high seas you're not hallucinating... it's just the tug "_____" promoting its children's TV program.

654

Safety Tip: If the bitter end of your chain anchor rode is secured with a length of line that is long enough to reach topsides while secured in the chain locker, then in the event of an emergency, it can be easily _____.

NAUTI-BENDER

Answers From
Page 217

646

**aground
12 meters**

647

starboard side

648

red left leaving

PHOTO: COURTESY OF TIARA YACHTS

You are cruising offshore on a beautiful, clear, sunny day. The sea state is calm, but large swells indicate the presence of a **distant** or **imminent** storm.

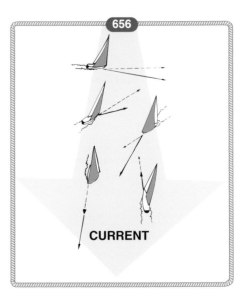

CURRENT

Currents at a 45° angle to the bow and stern affect course and speed at: **one-fourth**, **one-third**, or **one-half** the velocity of each.

NAUTI-BENDER
Answers From
Page 218

649
static electric

650
A: 3, B: 4,
C: 2, D: 1,
E: 5

651
stowaway
(If a little bread and water are
served, they will love it.)

Stand of the Tide: is the period when there is no discernible **vertical** or **horizontal** movement of water; i.e., top of *high water* or bottom of *low water*.

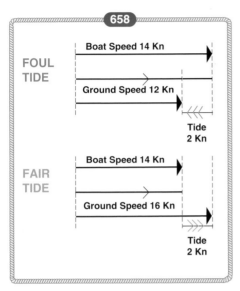

658

FOUL TIDE

Boat Speed 14 Kn

Ground Speed 12 Kn

Tide 2 Kn

FAIR TIDE

Boat Speed 14 Kn

Ground Speed 16 Kn

Tide 2 Kn

Typically, a **flood** or an **ebb** tide has the strongest current flow.

659

"Mackerel skies and mares' tails make tall ships carry low _____."

660

Slack Water: The period when there is no **horizontal** or **vertical** motion of the water.

NAUTI-BENDER

Answers From Page 219

652

1,000 boats/month

653

Theodore III

654

cut

661

PHOTO: COURTESY OF SWITLIK PARACHUTE COMPANY, INC.

**The Golden Rule of Life Raft Deployment:
Don't do it...** unless your feet are getting
_____ and you have to step _____ into the
raft!

662

HYPOTHERMIA TREATMENT DO'S AND DON'TS

A. Remove all of the victim's wet clothing.

B. Rub the victim's extremities or outer body to get circulation back.

C. Place the victim under blankets or preferably in a sleeping bag with warm (body temperature) towels applied to his or her groin, chest, neck and head.

D. Feed the patient alcohol, hot drinks, hot coffee, or other stimulants.

Proper treatment for hypothermia can speed recovery. Improper treatment can induce further damage or even death. Which, of the above re-warming treatments are "**do's**" and which are "**don'ts**"?

NAUTI-BENDER
Answers From
Page 220

655

distant storm

656

one-half
(plus or minus,
depending on direction)

657

vertical movement

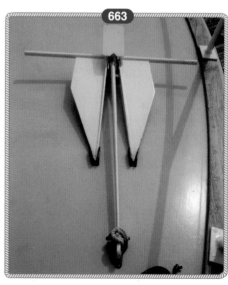

663

When not in use, anchors and other gear should be properly secured to avoid loss, potential crew injury, or boat damage by unexpected _____ action.

664

AVOIDING TROUBLE ON-THE-WATER

1. Don't take chances with weather.
2. Plan the trip with safety time margins and alternate routes.
3. Keep an orderly boat.
4. Be careful moving about the boat.
5. Wear a safety harness or life jacket if needed.
6. Don't stand on hatch covers, sails or lines.
7. Go forward on the leeward side.
8. Keep warm, dry, well fed and rested.
9. Be prepared, practice redundancy and don't panic.

Avoiding trouble while on-the-water requires good seamanship practices... **which of the above is incorrect**?

665

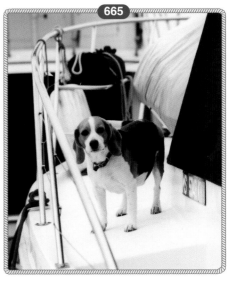

Keep Rufas Safe: Purchase a good pet PFD and keep it on him while at sea. Also, at night, it is a good idea to clip a safety _____ to the dog's PFD.

666

Battery compartments should always be well ventilated to: (A) **avoid carbon dioxide buildup**; (B) **ensure an adequate supply of oxygen for the battery's operation**; (C) **avoid accumulation of explosive vapors**.

NAUTI-BENDER
Answers From
Page 221

658
ebb tide

659
low sails

660
horizontal motion
(That is, there is no tidal current running in or out.)

In general, the length of your dock lines should be: (A) **bow line** = _____ x the beam's width; (B) **spring lines** = _____ x the overall length; and (C) **stern line** = _____ to _____ x the beam's width (add 5% for shrinkage).

The non-pliable characteristics of _____ line sometimes makes it difficult to use traditional fastening techniques and knots. The above "tucking" technique solves this problem.

NAUTI-BENDER
Answers From
Page 222

661
**feet are getting wet
step up into the raft**

662
**A: DO,
B: DON'T,   C: DO,
D: DON'T**

663
wave/wake action

If your dock lines are becoming stiff due to age or exposure to the sun, try soaking them overnight in a liquid _____ _____.

Polypropylene is better than nylon line for some applications. For example, it can be more easily "_____" as shown above. However, it is considerably less resistant to the sun's damaging ultraviolet rays.

_____ rope is best suited for a painter or ski tow-line because its buoyancy characteristics will keep it out of the propeller(s) when backing down.

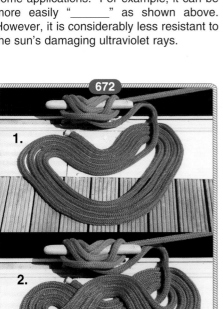

1.

2.

Some skippers keep their docklines as bristol as their boats. The above technique is referred to as the "_____- _____ flemish".

NAUTI-BENDER
Answers From
Page 223

664

7. Go forward on the ***windward side*** (avoid thrashing boom).

665

safety light

666

C: to avoid accumulation of explosive vapors

On what body of water is a compass almost useless?

"Returning from seaward", in general, is considered to be **clockwise** or **counter-clockwise** around the Atlantic, Gulf, and Pacific coasts.

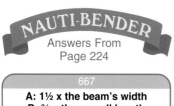

NAUTI-BENDER
Answers From
Page 224

667
A: 1½ x the beam's width
B: ¾ x the overall length
C: 1½ – 2 x the beam's width

668
polypropylene line

669
fabric softener

Oceans – the boater's playground – cover what percentage of the earth's surface... **60%**, **70%**, or **80%**? Which ocean is the largest: the **Antarctic**; **Arctic**; **Atlantic**; **Indian**; or the **Pacific**?

"Returning from Seaward" (buoys): is generally considered to be northerly and westerly on the Great Lakes, except on Lake _____ (considered southerly).

Entering a river from sea, your _____ chart ends. Who produces the charts for the rest of your voyage up the river?

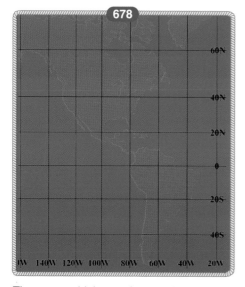

The most widely used coastal navigation charts utilize "_____ projection" to produce parallels of latitude and meridians of longitude that intersect at right angles.

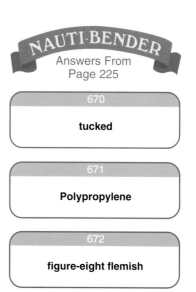

NAUTI-BENDER
Answers From
Page 225

670

tucked

671

Polypropylene

672

figure-eight flemish

Riding Out a Thunderstorm at Anchor: Set the anchor (use plenty of scope... 10:1 ratio) then apply just enough power with the engine to _____ _____ and *head up* into the storm.

Caught in a squall, which sail would normally come down first?

NAUTI-BENDER
Answers From
Page 226

673
a river

674
clockwise

675
70% of the earth's surface the Pacific

In thick fog, especially in congested shipping lanes, a dinghy should be towed behind the boat for _____ use in an emergency situation.

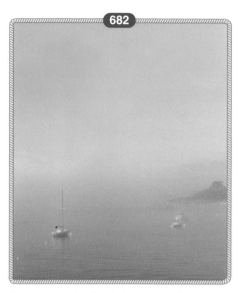

A pea-soup fog bank is approaching. You should: (A) **note your position on the chart**; (B) **plot a course to the nearest harbor**; (C) **attempt to outrun the fog to safety**; or (D) **all of the above**?

Sailing behind an isolated thunderstorm, there will be _____ wind.

Cruising in fog, **always** or **never** stand on your right-of-way per the rules of the road.

NAUTI-BENDER
Answers From
Page 227

676
Lake Michigan

677
NOAA: sea charts
Army Corps of Engineers: inland charts

678
Mercator projection

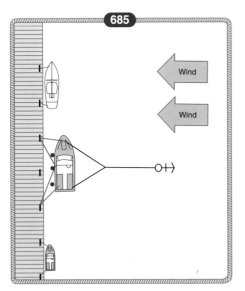

If a strong wind, waves, or wakes are banging your boat against the dock... set an anchor amidships, rig a bridle from the bow and stern and "_____" her away from the dock.

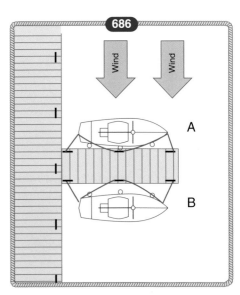

Which slip, "**A**" or "**B**", shown above, would be less strain on the boat and more comfortable for the crew in strong wind conditions?

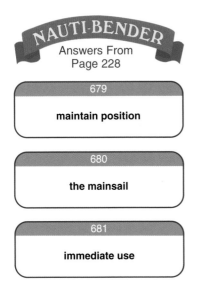

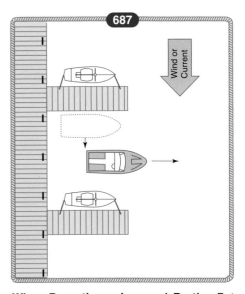

When Departing a Leeward Berth: Put the engine in _____, cast off all lines (bow and stern last) and when Mother Nature has helped the boat drift clear – motor out.

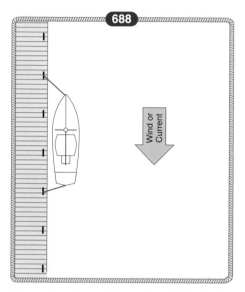

When departing, with your bow into wind or tidal current... should you leave **bow** or **stern** first?

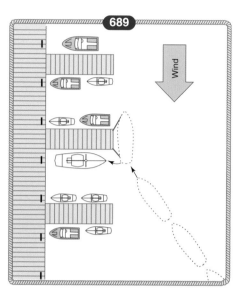

Docking With Poor Reverse Control: Maneuver to the end of the slip (bow into the wind); secure the boat with bow and stern lines; and then the crew can "_____" her in.

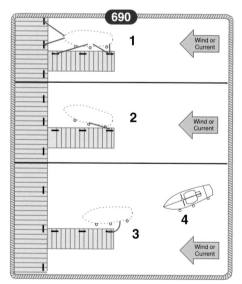

Departing with a strong wind/current from astern: With all lines on, go ahead slow with the rudder hard right. Cast off all lines except the _____ _____ _____ line, put the engine in neutral, cast off the _____, and back out.

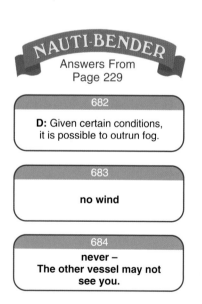

NAUTI-BENDER

Answers From
Page 229

682

D: Given certain conditions, it is possible to outrun fog.

683

no wind

684

never –
The other vessel may not see you.

The most obvious difference between a *yawl* and a *ketch* is that the aftermast is *stepped* **forward of** or **aft of** the rudder post in a yawl.

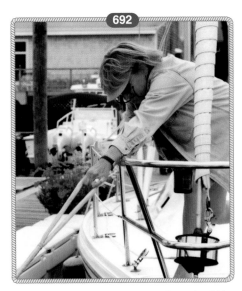

Line Handling Language: When the Skipper wants all lines secured, he/she will instruct the line handler (lest we captains forget... it's a tough job) to make the lines "_____ _____".

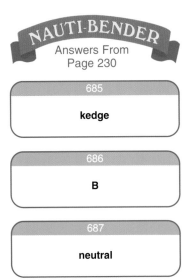

NAUTI-BENDER

Answers From
Page 230

685
kedge

686
B

687
neutral

PHOTO: COURTESY OF PACIFIC SEACRAFT YACHTS

Of the following mammal-related nautical terms, which one(s) would normally not be found on a boat: (A) "**cat**"; (B) "**mole**"; (C) "**dog**"; (D) "**donkey**"; and/or (E) "**dolphin**"?

Line Handling Language: When the skipper wants a line momentarily eased, to let the boat move slightly, he/she would instruct the line handler to "_____" the line.

When a sailboat loses headway while attempting to *come about*, it is said to be "_____ _____".

PHOTO: COURTESY OF GRADY WHITE BOATS

Multi-hulled sail or powerboats are referred to as "_____" or "_____".

NAUTI-BENDER
Answers From
Page 231

688
bow first

689
walk

690
after bow spring line spring

PHOTO: COURTESY OF SWITLIK PARACHUTE COMPANY

When deploying a life raft (calm weather), you secure the tether line to the boat and toss the raft overboard. The raft doesn't open up... why?

PHOTO: COURTESY OF THE U.S. COAST GUARD

When conditions warrant wearing a safety harness, remember to snap it on **before** going on _____ and keep it on **at all times** while on _____.

NAUTI-BENDER
Answers From
Page 232

691
aft of the rudder post

692
all fast

693
B: mole (a jetty or pier)
E: dolphin (cluster of pilings)

When boarding a dinghy, step aft if someone is forward, step forward if someone is aft, but **always** step into the "_____" of the boat.

Situation: You have a *MOB* and you have successfully thrown a life ring with a line attached to the victim. You're in high winds and heavy seas... remember, it is impossible for the *MOB* to hang on if the boat is travelling more than _____ mph.

A safety harness should be worn at any time when you begin to feel _____, or at night, during rough weather, sailing single-handedly, and/or when out of sight of other crew.

In every situation, the safety of the crew and the boat should be the Skipper's primary consideration. What two basic rules did the Skipper above disregard when returning from the mooring?

Answers From Page 233

694

surge the line

695

in irons

696

Catamarans or Trimarans

Generally speaking, the most favorable bottom for anchoring is **soft mud**, **rocky**, or a **mixture of mud and clay**.

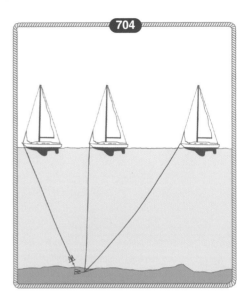

If the anchor won't break loose: cleat the rode when directly over the anchor, then proceed slowly on **the same** or **the opposite** course used initially when setting the anchor, until it breaks free.

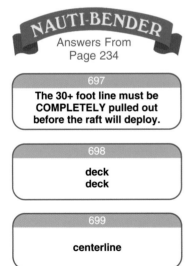

NAUTI-BENDER
Answers From Page 234

697
The 30+ foot line must be COMPLETELY pulled out before the raft will deploy.

698
deck
deck

699
centerline

Anchor Stuck: Take a strain on the anchor line (attach a float); tie a bowline around the anchor line and let it slip down around the anchor; then pull the release line in the _____ direction.

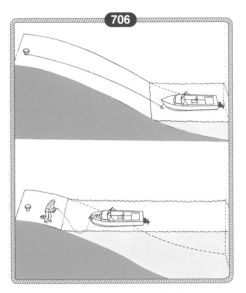

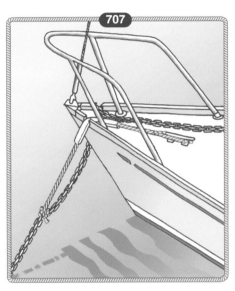

Retrieving a boat anchored off a beach in a flood tide is easily accomplished by rigging a "_____ _____" to the head of the anchor and proceeding as shown above.

On a boat with all-chain rodes, one should consider adding a nylon shock absorber or "_____ _____" in bad weather, or at rough anchorages.

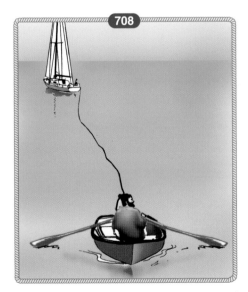

When laying out a "kedge" or second anchor, is it easier to row if the anchor rode is payed out from the **dinghy** or the **boat**?

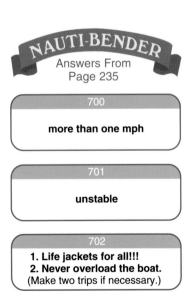

NAUTI-BENDER
Answers From
Page 235

700
more than one mph

701
unstable

702
1. Life jackets for all!!!
2. Never overload the boat.
(Make two trips if necessary.)

The sun is shining, the fish are jumping, and it's time to shove off. While preparing to get underway... **should you unplug the shore-power cord from the boat's inlet before the dock-receptacle, or vice versa?**

NAUTI-BENDER
Answers From
Page 236

703

a mixture of mud and clay

704

the opposite course

705

the opposite direction

Your boat's capacity plate gives the maximum load and _____ rating. When calculating the load, multiply the number of crew times 150 lbs; plus fuel (each gallon: gasoline 6.1 lbs; diesel 7.1 lbs); water (8.3 lbs/gallon); and gear.

A storm has been forecast. A friend of yours from the marina calls and requests that you move his boat out to the mooring. Why does a loud bell sound momentarily when you start the engine?

Do your bimini tie-downs vibrate in the wind or at high speed? To eliminate this problem, simply incorporate _____ _____ when rigging the tie-downs.

SEASICKNESS PREVENTION

1. Avoiding alcoholic beverages.
2. Avoiding greasy foods.
3. Avoiding exhaust fumes.
4. Keeping warm and dry.
5. Staying on deck, amidships.
6. Sitting down.
7. Drinking ginger ale.
8. Keeping mentally and physically active (steer the boat).
9. Focusing on the horizon.
10. Lying down or standing upright.

Which of the above **does not** prevent sea-sickness?

Freshwater Boaters: To preserve the _____ _____ of your inland waters... please remove any plant material from your boat/trailer before proceeding to another boating area.

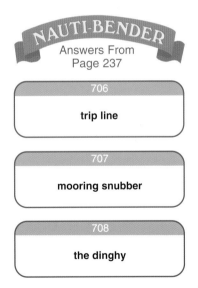

NAUTI-BENDER
Answers From
Page 237

706

trip line

707

mooring snubber

708

the dinghy

PHOTO: COURTESY OF CATALINA YACHTS, BY TOM VIOLAND

715

While under sail, you begin to experience excessive heel and weather helm in addition to a constant need to luff, all of which usually indicate a need to _____ or _____ _____.

PHOTO: COURTESY OF BOSTON WHALER BOATS, BY ROBERT HOLLAND

716

While exploring a new lake, all of a sudden your engine bogs down and the speedometer quits working... what is the obvious problem and the easiest remedy?

NAUTI-BENDER
Answers From Page 238

709

The boat's shore-power receptacle first (to avoid dropping a "hot" wire in the water)

710

boat's maximum power rating (Note: a six-pack of beer equals five pounds.)

711

The boat's engine warning system is being tested.

717

When offshore, keeping on course is made easier by picking and steering toward: a distant landmark; another fixed object; or a _____ at night that coincides with the desired course.

PHOTO: COURTESY OF SEA TOW

When going aground, the proper procedure is to gun the engine(s) astern immediately...
True or **False**?

PHOTO: COURTESY OF BERTRAM YACHTS

The quickest and safest way to shut down a runaway diesel engine is to cut off the: (A) **air**; (B) **fuel**; or (C) **electrical supply**.

PHOTO: COURTESY OF THE U.S. COAST GUARD

When towing, always start off gently and gradually build way until you have reached a moderate towing speed – never exceed the disabled boat's _____ speed.

NAUTI-BENDER
Answers From
Page 239

712
three twists

713
sitting down
(the worst position)

714
ecological balance (The above shown "milfoil" weed has invaded most of the northeast.)

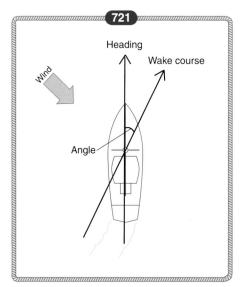

"_____ *angle*" is the angle between the course steered and the direction actually made good through the water. This effect is typically caused by the wind or sea motion.

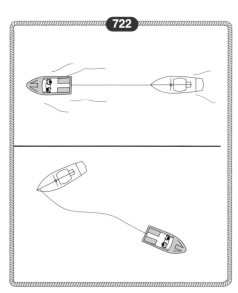

A towboat is considered "_____" when the forward motion of the disabled boat carries it past the towboat and causes the towboat to swing around in the opposite direction of travel.

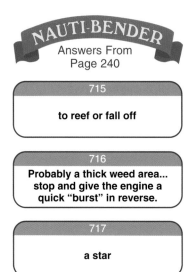

NAUTI-BENDER
Answers From
Page 240

715

to reef or fall off

716

Probably a thick weed area... stop and give the engine a quick "burst" in reverse.

717

a star

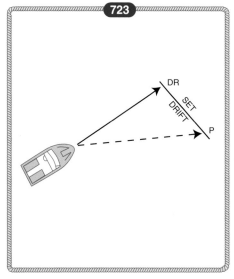

A combination of "set" and "drift" is referred to as "_____".

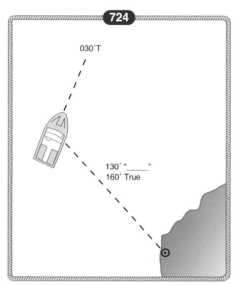

724

030°T

130° "_____"
160° True

"_____ _____" is the direction relative to the fore- and aft-line of a vessel expressed in degrees.

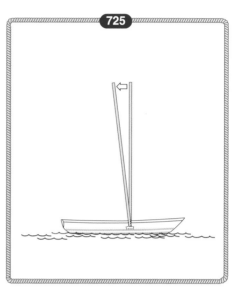

725

"_____" is the angle of the mast, stern, or stem. "_____" is the curvature of the deck as seen from the side.

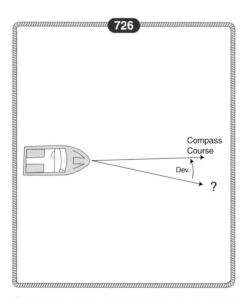

726

Compass
Course

Dev.

?

Compass course plus or minus deviation amounts will equal the _____ course.

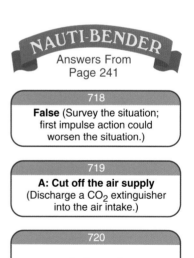

NAUTI-BENDER
Answers From
Page 241

718
False (Survey the situation; first impulse action could worsen the situation.)

719
A: Cut off the air supply
(Discharge a CO_2 extinguisher into the air intake.)

720
hull speed

PHOTO: COURTESY OF PURSUIT BOATS, BY FOREST JOHNSON

Cruising offshore you encounter a leak in your hydraulic steering system. After repairing the leak, which of the following can be temporarily substituted for the lost hydraulic fluid: **fresh water**; **sea water**; **beer**; or **all of the above**?

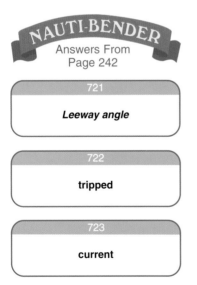

NAUTI-BENDER
Answers From
Page 242

721
Leeway angle

722
tripped

723
current

If your outboard engine should inadvertently fall overboard and is retrieved, it should be stored: **upside down**; **in the sun**; or **underwater** for several hours before being repaired.

After washing down the boat, pouring **a little** of the excess soapy water into the bilge accomplishes two objectives: it helps keep the bilge clean, plus it _____ any minor amounts of fuel or engine oil that may have accumulated.

First golden rule of working on inboard engines: lay a cloth or a blanket under the work area to prevent dropped _____ and _____ from falling into the bilge.

Spring Commissioning: One important check, often overlooked, is checking the auto-float switch(es) on the bilge pump(s) before _____ the boat!

PHOTO: COURTESY OF HUNTER YACHTS

Do your partially used cans of varnish and boat paint develop a "skin" on the top of the liquid while stored? Suggestion... simply store the cans _____-_____.

NAUTI-BENDER
Answers From
Page 243

724
Relative bearing

725
Rake
Sheer

726
magnetic

733

The navigation rules are not explicit, however, it may be inferred that a boat emerging from a slip or berth **does** or **does not** have the right-of-way. What sound signals should the above vessel sound before backing out?

734

Cruising up a large river, you encounter a tug with a barge. The tug's skipper says he would like you to come up on his "*two whistle*". On which side should you pass?

NAUTI-BENDER

Answers From
Page 244

727

all of the above

728

stored underwater
(to prevent oxidation)

729

disperses (For environmental considerations, this procedure should only be done occasionally.)

735

Approaching an obscured bend, a vessel should indicate its presence by sounding one prolonged blast _____ to _____ second(s) in length.

You are approaching a drawbridge that will open any time upon request. What signal should be sounded to request that the bridge be opened?

Which waterborne vessel(s) is/are not required to display the usual arrangement of red, green or white lights: (A) **seaplanes**; (B) **submarines**; (C) **air-cushion boats**; and/or (D) **cruising cars**?

Sailboats, when under sail, are not required to use maneuvering navigation sound signals (passing or overtaking) – **True** or **False**?

NAUTI-BENDER
Answers From
Page 245

730

parts and tools

731
launching the boat
(Also, don't forget the drain plug.)

732

upside-down

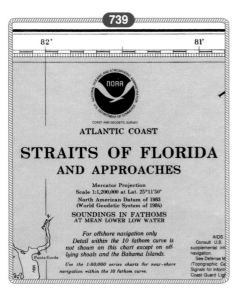

739

ATLANTIC COAST

STRAITS OF FLORIDA
AND APPROACHES

Mercator Projection
Scale 1:1,200,000 at Lat. 25°11'50"
North American Datum of 1983
(World Geodetic System of 1984)

SOUNDINGS IN FATHOMS
AT MEAN LOWER LOW WATER

For offshore navigation only
Detail within the 10 fathom curve is
not shown on this chart except on off-
lying shoals and the Bahama Islands.

AIDS
Consult U.S.
supplemental inf
navigation.
See Defense M
/Topographic Ce
Signals for inform
Coast Guard Ligt

Use the 1:80,000 series charts for near-shore
navigation within the 10 fathom curve.

Punta Gorda

Caution: Inshore charts typically show depths in _____ and offshore charts often show depths in _____ or _____.

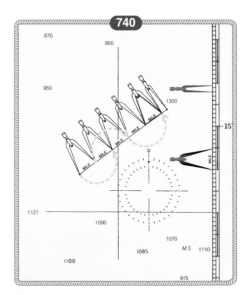

740

How many feet are there in a nautical mile: (A) **5,280**; (B) **5,980**; (C) **6,076**; or (D) **6,650** feet?

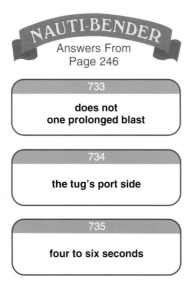

NAUTI-BENDER
Answers From
Page 246

733

does not
one prolonged blast

734

the tug's port side

735

four to six seconds

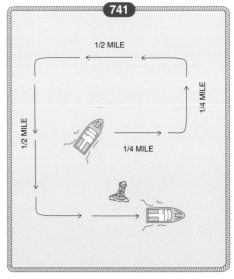

741

1/2 MILE

1/4 MILE

1/2 MILE

1/4 MILE

Finding a Buoy in Thick Fog: Stop where you think _____ _____ _____, then search in a square pattern of half-mile legs until you find it.

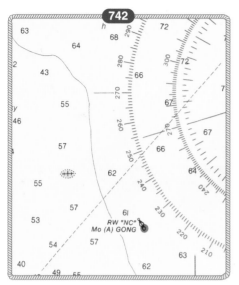

Referring to the buoy symbol shown above: the line in the diamond indicates red and white _____ _____; the little circle at the top indicates a _____ _____; and "GONG" indicates _____-_____ _____.

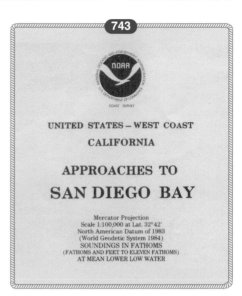

A scale of 1:100,000 on a NOAA chart indicates that 1 inch on the chart equals: (A) **100,000 miles**; (B) **100,000 yards**; (C) **100,000 inches**; or (D) **100,000 feet** on land.

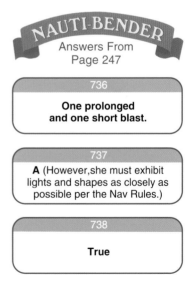

Answers From Page 247

736

One prolonged and one short blast.

737

A (However, she must exhibit lights and shapes as closely as possible per the Nav Rules.)

738

True

The Rule of Threes: allows for a quick approximation of distance traveled (in yards) in three minutes at any multiple of three knots (add two zeroes). For example, how far would you travel in six minutes at nine knots?

Docking Tip: To facilitate a quick tie-up with one person jumping on the dock while handling both the bow and stern line simultaneously... rig a stern line that is six feet longer than the _____ _____ _____.

A dock line can be easily tightened or "_____ _____" by stepping down on the line, while it's "checked" at the cleat and then, in one quick motion, taking up the slack while removing your foot.

NAUTI-BENDER
Answers From Page 248

739
feet **fathoms or meters** (A fathom equals 6 feet.)

740
C: 6,076 feet

741
think it should be

A "_____" line is ideal for single-handed docking. Loop the eye over the onboard cleat and coil the line ready for use... when alongside, proceed as shown above.

When tying-up, run lines and/or position the boat to achieve a "_____ lead" through the chock to reduce chafing.

When docking, a line handler inadvertently drops a line in the water. What should the Skipper's first action be?

At crowded marinas, open cleats are rare. So as not to disturb your neighbor's lines and vice versa, simply run your lines under the neighbor's and secure with a _____ as shown above.

NAUTI-BENDER
Answers From
Page 249

742
vertical stripes
spherical topmark
wave-actuated gong

743
C: 100,000 inches

744
1,800 yards
(2 X 900 = 1,800 yards)

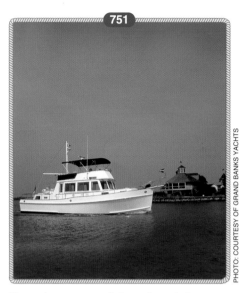

PHOTO: COURTESY OF GRAND BANKS YACHTS

The above vessel is referred to as a "_____".

PHOTO: COURTESY OF BOSTON WHALER BOATS

You're pulling your brother on a wakeboard and he goes "fakey". Should you: (A) **rush him to the nearest psycho ward**; (B) **report the incident to the local marine authorities**; or (C) **admire his wakeboarding skills**?

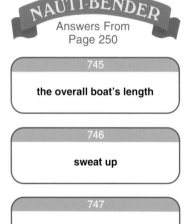

NAUTI-BENDER
Answers From Page 250

745

the overall boat's length

746

sweat up

747

a breast line

Inveterate sailors proclaim for a vessel to be "lucky", she should be named after (A) **a bird**, (B) **a fish**, (C) **the captain's significant other**, or (D) **a famous place** (pick two).

754

In the winter, when cold air (below 10° F) blows "off the land" over sea water, a steamy fog may form what seamen call "_____ _____".

PHOTO: BY VINCE TIBBITTS, GLOUCESTER, MA

755

When towing, it is good practice to periodically **shorten** or **lengthen** the tow rope to avoid chafing... referred to as "freshening the _____".

PHOTO: COURTESY OF THE U.S. COAST GUARD

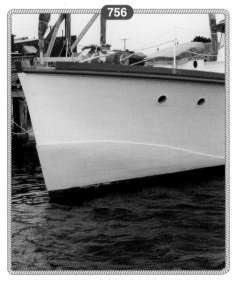

756

Sometimes, when a pleasure boat has been on a long cruise, a greenish stain forms on the bow and is referred to as a "_____".

NAUTI-BENDER
Answers From Page 251

748
fair lead (If unable to achieve a fair lead, use chafing gear as shown above.)

749
stop the propeller(s)
(until the line is retrieved)

750
bowline

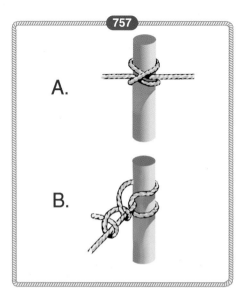

Make Fast to a Piling: Both methods shown above will work. However, what advantage does "**B**" have over "**A**"?

A *bowline in a bight*, shown above, is useful for hoisting someone back onboard (one leg each loop) or for creating a simple "_____" which can be used to make a lashing more taut.

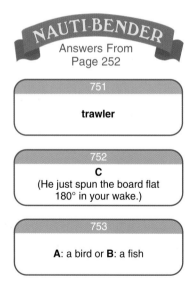

NAUTI-BENDER
Answers From
Page 252

751

trawler

752

C
(He just spun the board flat 180° in your wake.)

753

A: a bird or **B**: a fish

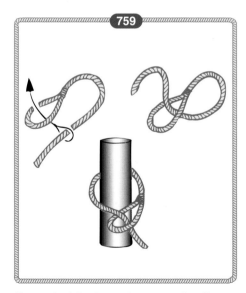

If your dock line's *eye* is too small to fit over a piling, thread the "_____ _____" through the *eye* to make a noose.

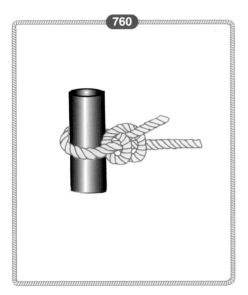

The most popular method of attaching a line to a spar, stanchion, or a ring is with two "_____ _____", as shown above.

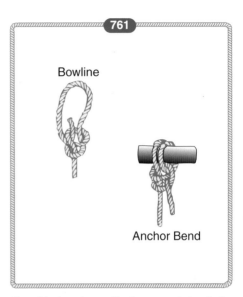

Considering that a line's strength is diminished in varying degrees when tied with different knots... would a **bowline** or **anchor bend** be preferable when rigging a tow-line to a boat's bow eye?

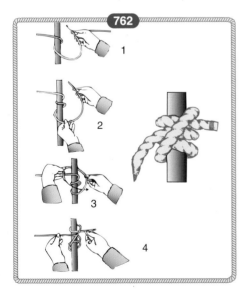

The "_____ hitch" is unique in that when tied to a vertical object (a mast, a stanchion, a line, or a cable) it won't slip downward under strain and can easily be adjusted upward.

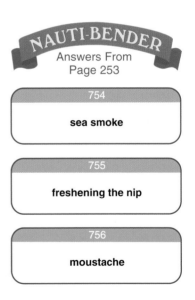

NAUTI-BENDER
Answers From
Page 253

754
sea smoke

755
freshening the nip

756
moustache

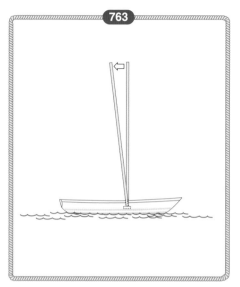

763

"**Raking**" is the bending of the mast aft (2° to 5°) to change the shape of the mainsail, normally done when sailing _____ to the _____.

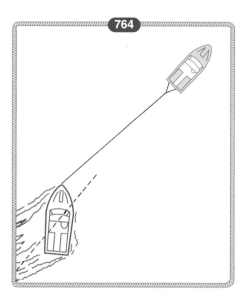

764

Your boat is being towed and begins to yaw excessively. Which of the following steps will most effectively reduce the yawing: (A) **shifting weight aft**; (B) **a reduction in towing speed**; or (C) **lengthening the tow rope**?

NAUTI-BENDER
Answers From
Page 254

757

"A" may slip and jam under load, "B" will not.

758

purchase

759

the standing part
(will be difficult to get loose under strain and may slide when slack.)

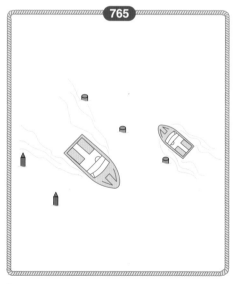

765

In some circumstances (thick fog, heavy ship traffic, etc.), it may be wise to run just _____ the edge of a well buoyed, deep-draft ship channel.

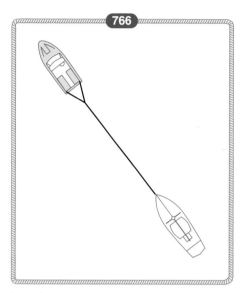

Lengthening a tow rope generally **decreases** or **increases** the maneuverability of the towboat.

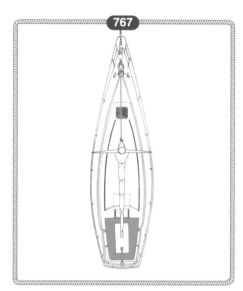

Some boats do not have heavy enough forward cleats for towing in rough seas. In this situation, a doubled or trebled "_____ _____" should be rigged as shown above.

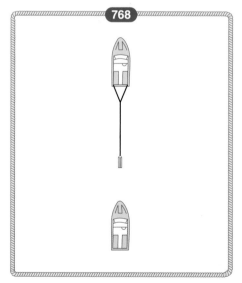

When cruising with another yacht, the above technique (towing a fender or old life jacket) would be quite useful in thick _____.

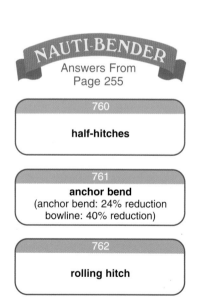

NAUTI-BENDER
Answers From
Page 255

760
half-hitches

761
anchor bend
(anchor bend: 24% reduction
bowline: 40% reduction)

762
rolling hitch

What is the most important step in launching a boat in "slings" with a crane?

Using your "head"... to avoid unnecessary sanitary work and bad odors... "**Gentlemen: Please Be Seated!**" To avoid clogs, use no more than _____ squares of toilet tissue per flush.

NAUTI-BENDER
Answers From
Page 256

763

close to the wind

764

A: shifting weight aft

765

outside
(check the charts first!)

PHOTO: COURTESY OF PAT PIPER, ANNAPOLIS, MD

When purchasing or replacing boat trailer tires, always select tires designated "**ST**"; "**P**"; or "**LT**". These tires are of a heavier construction, designed to meet additional load requirements.

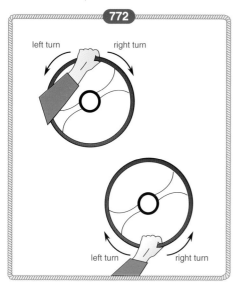

Backing boat trailers can be made easier by the placement of your hand... on the _____ of the wheel for going ahead and on the _____ for backing up (as shown above).

Sophisticated racing sails are typically made of _____ or _____.

PHOTO: COURTESY OF ALDEN YACHTS

Most recreational boats utilize main and jib sails made of _____ and spinnakers made of _____.

NAUTI-BENDER
Answers From
Page 257

766
increases

767
towing bridle

768
thick fog

Using obscene, indecent, or profane language during radio communication is punishable by a _____ fine, imprisonment for _____ years, or both.

It is dangerous and against federal law to have legs hanging over the side of a boat – **True** or **False**?

NAUTI-BENDER
Answers From
Page 258

769
The slings must be properly positioned or the boat may suffer structural damage.

770
six squares

771
ST: Special Trailer
P: Passenger Car
LT: Light Truck

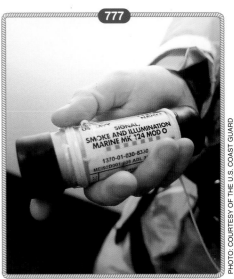

Marine flares expire in **36**, **42**, or **48** months. Since you have plenty of extra expired spares onboard, and it is illegal to practice launch flares... **how do you dispose of them properly**?

While you're watching the annual Dory Boat races, your engine quits. You drift into the path of one of the racers... although the racers divert, one scrapes your boat. Who's at fault?

Operating a vessel while intoxicated is a federal offense subject to civil penalty not to exceed $_____ or criminal penalty not to exceed $_____, and/or _____ year(s) imprisonment.

PHOTO: COURTESY OF THE U.S. COAST GUARD

After an unsuccessful attempt at contacting another boat on Channel 9, you should wait _____ minutes before another attempt and, after three attempts you should wait _____ minutes before resuming.

NAUTI-BENDER
Answers From Page 259

772

top – for going ahead
bottom – for backing up

773

Mylar or Kevlar

774

main and jib – dacron
spinnakers – nylon

261

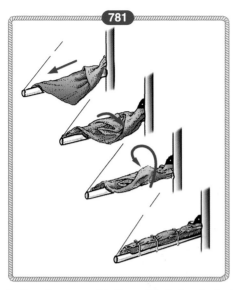

In the above graphic the sail is being **furled** or **flaked** for storage. The "_____" or "_____" are tied every four or five feet with a slipped "_____" or "_____" knot.

The "_____", is a modern anchor that holds **poorly**, **adequately**, or **well** in most bottoms?

NAUTI-BENDER
Answers From
Page 260

775
$10,000 **two years imprisonment**

776
True

777
42 months; Local CG Flotillas **may accept them; or dispose** **at a hazardous waste site.**

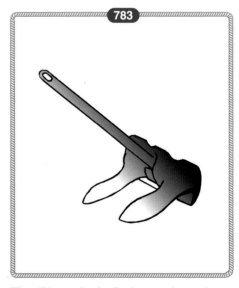

The "Navy Anchor" shown above is an excellent anchor for most sized pleasure craft: **True** or **False**?

784

The "_____" anchor is good for most bottoms and well suited for hanging from a "_____".

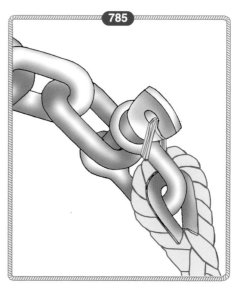

785

After mooring or anchor-rode shackles have been tightened, "_____" the shackle pin with copper wire, small stuff, or a plastic tie wrap.

786

The "_____" or "_____" anchor (shown above) is good for anchoring in _____ but not the best choice for all-around use.

What day shape would the above vessel display to indicate that she was anchored?

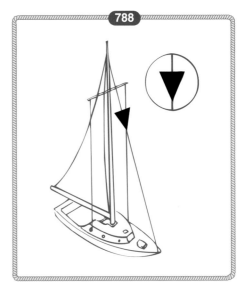

The vessel above is displaying a day shape indicating she is _____ _____.

NAUTI-BENDER
Answers From
Page 262

781
furled
gaskets or stops
reef or *square knot*

782
Danforth
holds well

783
false (To hold a 25' boat would require a 350 lb Navy anchor vs. a 15 lb Danforth.)

The vessel above is displaying a day shape indicating she is _____.

The above vessel is displaying a day shape indicating she is _____ _____ _____.

A buoy or marker's shape **always** indicates its color – **True** or **False**?

Cruising in open water, the mate sights a float with a small flag in the distance, indicating the presence of a: **fish net**; **race marker**; **sunken vessel**; **diver**; or **any one of the above**?

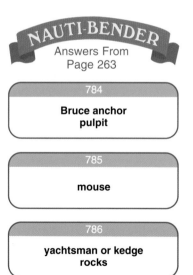

NAUTI-BENDER
Answers From
Page 263

784
**Bruce anchor
pulpit**

785
mouse

786
**yachtsman or kedge
rocks**

793

Cloud Weather Forecaster: When puffy cumulus clouds over water quickly become higher than they are wide, this change indicates: **continued good weather**; **changing weather**; or **the possibility of severe winds and lightning**.

794

PHOTO: COURTESY OF THE U.S. COAST GUARD

Generally speaking, the most destructive storms occurring on the Great Lakes usually come from the: **northeast/east**; **southwest/west**; **northwest/north**; or **southeast/south**.

NAUTI-BENDER
Answers From
Page 264

787

a single black ball

788

under power

789

fishing
(two triangles pointed together
or basket)

795

Reading the Wind: How do you know when a rainstorm is ending? Northeast-to-south winds shifting to the **east** or **west** usually signal a storm's break.

Fog forms when the temperature and the _____ are the same.

When a full moon occurs at your geographical location... **what time is high tide**?

Small craft warnings are set when the wind speed is between _____ to _____ knots.

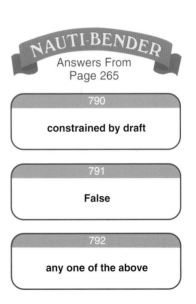

NAUTI-BENDER
Answers From
Page 265

790

constrained by draft

791

False

792

any one of the above

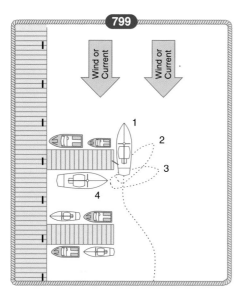

When docking in strong wind, tidal current, or tight quarters, let the dock lines do the _____ to minimize stress/embarrassing situations for the skipper and crew.

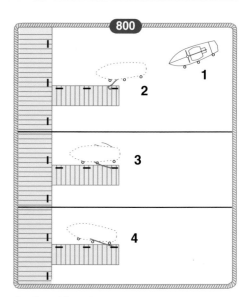

Spring Line Arrival: Approach the pier slowly at approximately a 20° angle. Shift into neutral and attach the spring line. Apply a "burst of power" in reverse to stop the boat's forward motion. Go ahead slow, rudder hard _____.

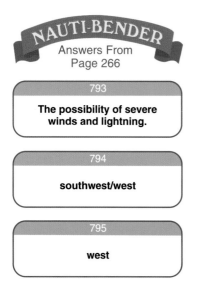

NAUTI-BENDER
Answers From
Page 266

793

The possibility of severe winds and lightning.

794

southwest/west

795

west

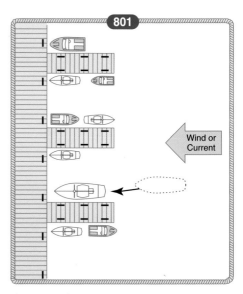

Docking Stern To the Wind (assuming the vessel has poor reverse control): Coast into the slip in neutral, and slow the boat's forward momentum with the _____ spring and the _____ line.

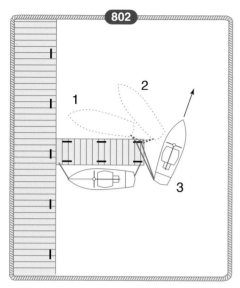

Spring-line departures from difficult berths can be made easier by rigging the spring as a "_____" line.

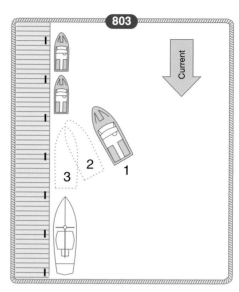

To "walk" a single-screw vessel sideways into a tight slip (assuming a fairly strong tidal current), hold her steady against current by _____ the throttle while easing the bow over.

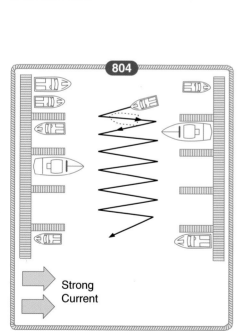

Strong
Current

To avoid being set side-to a strong current and "_____ _____" onto the other boats, one should utilize a series of back and forth maneuvers as shown above.

NAUTI·BENDER

Answers From
Page 267

796
dewpoint

797
midnight (Full moon tides always occur around the same hour ± 60 minutes.)

798
18 to 33 knots

805

806

Going full-ahead (inboard single-screw vessel, right-hand propeller), if the engine is put astern with hard-left rudder, the stern will:
(A) **swing slowly, then quickly to port**; or
(B) **swing to starboard until headway is lost, then to port**.

Most trailerable boats have a bow eye which is excellent for attaching a _____ _____ or mooring _____.

NAUTI-BENDER
Answers From
Page 268

799
work

800
right
(or away from the pier)

801
aft spring and bow line

807

When approaching a closed drawbridge from the up-current side... why should the Skipper hover well above the commitment point?

When towing at sea or in rough waters, the towline should be as _____ as possible while keeping the two boats "in-step". In quiet or protected waters, the towline should be as _____ as possible to allow for better control.

When entering an unfamiliar harbor without a chart at low tide, could you safely proceed by following: (A) **another boat**; (B) **lobster pots**; or (C) **a line of moorings**?

While bucking a very strong tidal current, you pass through a drawbridge. The water is choppy and confused... how should you proceed to safely maneuver through the bridge?

NAUTI-BENDER
Answers From
Page 269

802
slip line

803
adjusting

804
set down

When retrieving the anchor, what term is used to indicate that the anchor has cleared the bottom?

A pile of stones built in a symmetrical or non-symmetrical form is sometimes used as a lighted navigational aid and is referred to as a "_____".

NAUTI-BENDER
Answers From
Page 270

805

B: swing to starboard until headway is lost, then to port

806

tow line
mooring pendant

807

The current will increase through the bridge and may suck the boat into trouble.

On many lakes, a temporary (a few minutes to several hours) rise or fall of water may occur and is referred to as "_____". This fluctuation is typically caused by sudden changes in barometric pressure or strong winds.

When a boat jumps a wake at high speed... is the boat's prop **cavitating** or **ventilating**? (This maneuver could be potentially damaging to the boat and its crew and is not recommended.)

A line used to tow or tie up a dinghy or a tender is called the "_____".

Floating Wreckage/Cargo: "_____" is cargo deliberately thrown overboard; "_____" is gear or cargo thrown overboard marked with a buoy for later recovery; "_____" is wreckage and cargo from a sinking.

NAUTI-BENDER

Answers From
Page 271

808

long – rough waters
short – quiet waters

809

A: May not have local knowledge
B: May have been set at high tide
C: Safest approach

810

Aggressively adjust the throttle(s) as needed to maintain course and headway.

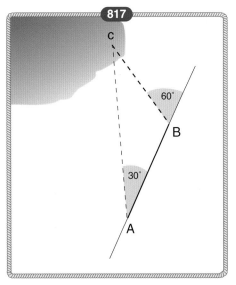

The above illustrates a simple method for calculating distance (A to B = B to C) using *relative bearings* and is called "*doubling* _____ _____ _____ _____ _____."

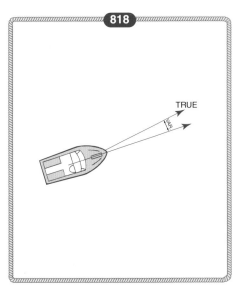

Your "true" course plus or minus variation amounts will equal your "_____" course.

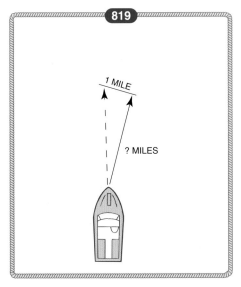

A 5° course error will result in being one mile off course after advancing: **5.7**; **8.2**; or **11.5** miles.

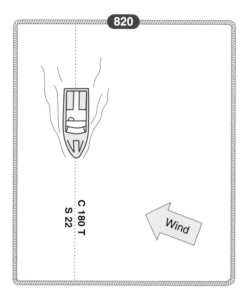

You're proceeding on a course of 180° true at a speed of 22 knots; the apparent wind is from 70° off the port bow at 20 knots. What is the direction/ speed of the true wind?

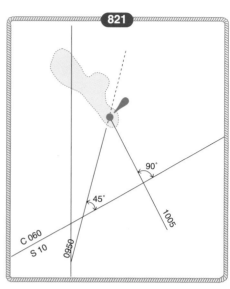

Using the "doubling the angle on the bow" method, **what is the distance to the buoy at 1005 hrs.**?

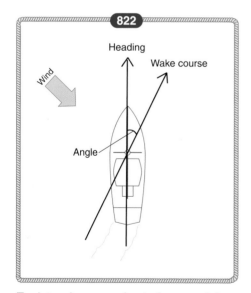

To determine approximate *leeway* – take a bearing of the wake your vessel is making and subtract it from the _____ of the course being steered.

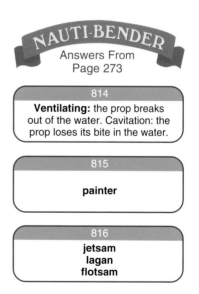

NAUTI-BENDER
Answers From
Page 273

814
Ventilating: the prop breaks out of the water. Cavitation: the prop loses its bite in the water.

815
painter

816
jetsam
lagan
flotsam

PHOTO: COURTESY OF THE U.S. COAST GUARD

The Four Vital Actions Required After Boarding a Life Raft: CUT the _____ line; STREAM the _____ _____; CLOSE the _____ and _____; and MAINTAIN the raft (bailing, inflating, checking for leaks, etc.).

PHOTO: COURTESY OF THE U.S. COAST GUARD

In the event of a collision, the first steps should include: determine the extent of the damage; effect repairs; don life jackets; and _____ the pumps.

NAUTI-BENDER
Answers From Page 274

817
doubling the angle on the bow

818
magnetic

819
11.5 miles

PHOTO: COURTESY OF BOSTON WHALER BOATS

When thick fog develops, it is good practice that all crew and passengers don lifejackets, and have all _____ equipment ready for use in an emergency.

PHOTO: COURTESY OF THE U.S. COAST GUARD

826

We have all witnessed and made bone-head mistakes on-the-water and have survived not to repeat them. However, the above is the most _____ adult-supervised activity we have ever seen.

PHOTO: COURTESY OF THE U.S. COAST GUARD, BY: AL EMGE

827

You're in a sinking situation without radio communications. After firing off several distress flares you observe three white flares far off in the distance... what does this mean?

828

"**Fend Off**": to push a boat clear or prevent violent contact with another boat, dock, or object by using: (A) **hands/legs**; (B) **boat hook**; (C) **a fender**; or (D) **all of the above**.

NAUTI-BENDER
Answers From
Page 275

820

51° at 24.2 knots

821

Dist. off $= \dfrac{10 \times 15}{60} = $ **2.5 miles**

822

reciprocal

829

If a vessel is carrying sails made of six oz. sailcloth, it means that a rectangle of the cloth measuring _____ x _____ inches will weigh six ounces.

PHOTO: BY JOHN SNYDER, NORTH CONWAY, NH

830

Assuming you've accidentally pumped a small amount of fuel overboard while taking on bunkers... you should immediately spray some Joy dishwashing liquid on the spill to disperse it – **True** or **False**?

NAUTI-BENDER
Answers From
Page 276

823
CUT the **painter** line
STREAM the **sea anchor**
Close the **doors and canopy**

824
man the pumps

825
safety equipment

831

QUESTION: SUBMITTED BY VINCE TIBBITTS, GLOUCESTER, MA

In rough anchorages, flexible _____-_____ hose can be cut vertically and placed at pressure points to avoid chafing your boat and/or the shore power line.

If it is hard to maintain a straight course at cruising speed, trim can be maintained by adjusting the transom drive's "_____-_____", located under the activation plate.

A 1½" hole located two feet below the water line will admit _____ gallons of water-per-minute. (It has not been estimated how many gallons-per-minute a frightened man with a bucket can remove.)

PHOTO: COURTESY OF THE U.S. COAST GUARD

Want another year out of your old boat cover? Where grommets have torn out, press an old golf ball against the inside of the cover, and then secure the outside with a _____ hitch, followed by _____ hitches.

NAUTI-BENDER
Answers From
Page 277

826
dangerous!!! (Major potential prop hazard and carbon monoxide poisioning risk.)

827
Your signal has been seen and assistance is forthcoming.

828
B and C
(It's very dangerous to use hands or legs.)

Winter Lay-up Tip: In those interior areas that are prone to mildew, strategically place a few boxes of **cat litter**, **soap powder**, or **baking soda** to absorb moisture and odors.

Outboard Winterization: The oil and filter in a **two-** or **four-stroke** engine should be changed each fall. Dirty oil contains acids that can ruin bearings during long-term inactivity.

NAUTI-BENDER
Answers From Page 278

829

28½ x 36 inches

830

False: most dispersants are harmful to sea life
(use an oil-absorbent pad)

831

flexible bilge-pump hose

Outboard Winterization: Gear case oil should be changed each fall. If water has entered, the oil will look _____; it could freeze and expand, damaging seals or cracking the case itself.

Outboard Winterization: Top off the fuel tank and add the correct amount of fuel sta-bilizer, then **run the engine for ten min-utes**, or, **drain the fuel system** to prevent gum or varnish formation.

Winter Layup: Be especially careful when shrink-wrapping around the: (A) **wind-shield**; (B) **the wheelhouse enclosure**; (C) **varnished trim**; or (D) **the fuel vent**.

Outboard Winterization: After "fogging" the engine, new spark plugs should be installed so she will be ready for the first cruise next spring – **True** or **False**?

NAUTI-BENDER

Answers From
Page 279

832

mini-rudder

833

70 gallons
(What is the capacity
of your bilge pump(s)?)

834

**clove hitch
half hitches**

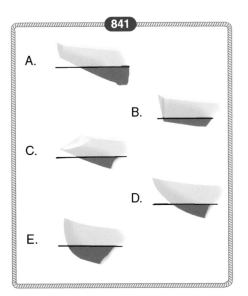

Stern Design: Identify the stern designs in "**A**", "**B**", "**C**", "**D**" and "**E**" shown above.

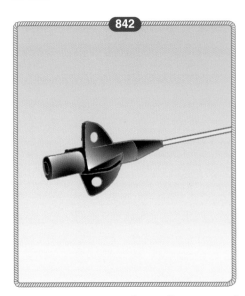

The "_____ _____", a distance and speed measuring device, which is towed, registers revolutions and records in miles and tenths of miles.

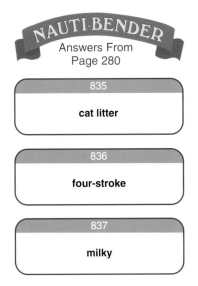

NAUTI-BENDER
Answers From
Page 280

835

cat litter

836

four-stroke

837

milky

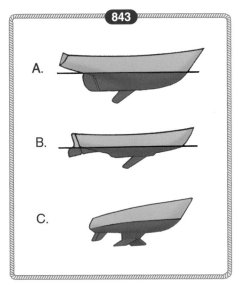

Identify the keel designs as shown in "**A**", "**B**", and "**C**" above.

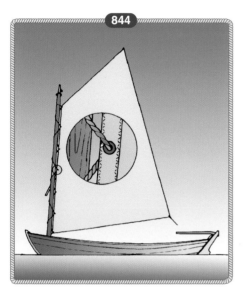

844

To "_____" a line is to lead it through an opening (an eye, block, thimble, etc.).

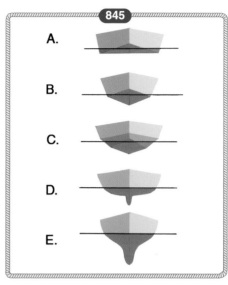

845

A.

B.

C.

D.

E.

Bottom Design: Identify the bottom designs shown in "**A**", "**B**", "**C**", "**D**", and "**E**" above.

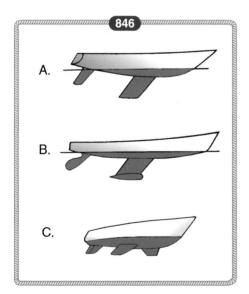

846

A.

B.

C.

Identify the keel designs shown in "**A**", "**B**," and "**C**" shown above.

NAUTI-BENDER
Answers From
Page 281

838

run the engine (Treated fuel is to remain in the system, especially fuel-injected engines.)

839

D: (The heat from the torch can ignite the venting fumes.)

840

False: The old plugs should be used so the fogging oil doesn't foul the new plugs.

847

One method to "refloat" your boat after running aground is to set a "_____" anchor and "_____" her over to reduce her draft.

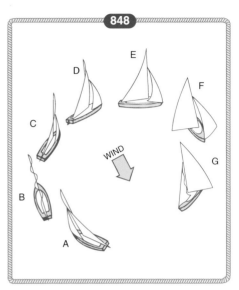

848

Which of the vessels shown above is on a beam-reach (port tack)?

NAUTI-BENDER
Answers From
Page 282

841
A: Counter   B: Transom
C: Reverse Counter
D: Canoe   E: Double Ender

842

Patent Log

843
A: *keel/centerboard*
B: *drop or swing keel*
C: *winged keel*

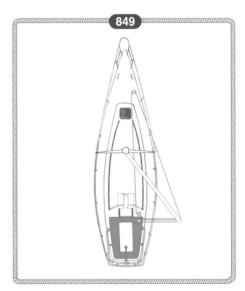

849

To prevent an accidental jibe while sailing downwind, rig a "_____ _____".

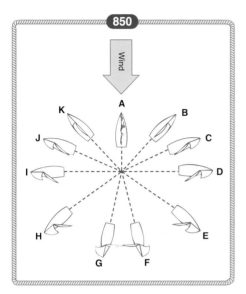

Which vessel shown above is on a close-hauled starboard tack?

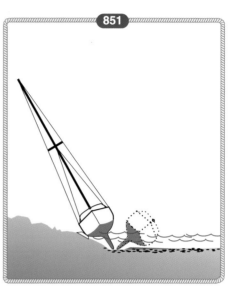

A grounded boat should be "_____" over on the side away from rising water, otherwise she may be flooded by an incoming tide.

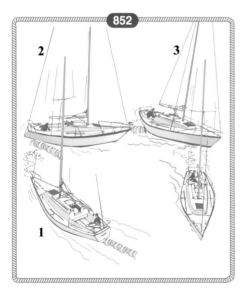

To turn in a tight circle (inboard, right-handed prop): **1.** Apply a burst of power ahead, with hard _____ rudder. **2.** Apply a burst of power astern with hard _____ rudder. **3.** Keep her turning with another burst **ahead** or **astern**.

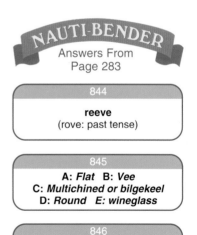

NAUTI-BENDER
Answers From
Page 283

844

reeve
(rove: past tense)

845

A: *Flat* B: *Vee*
C: *Multichined or bilgekeel*
D: *Round* E: *wineglass*

846

A: fin
B: bulb
C: twin

Double the Life of Your Docklines: When they start getting worn, try reversing them end-for-end so the chafing point changes. This procedure is sometimes referred to as "_____".

If your dock line is not quite long enough to tie up in the traditional manner, a _____ hitch and a "slippery" _____ hitch can be utilized as shown above.

NAUTI-BENDER
Answers From
Page 284

847
kedge anchor **heel her over**

848
D

849
a boom preventer

Line Nomenclature: Identify "**A**", "**B**", and "**C**" shown above. How long is a "hank" of line?

Some docks don't have cleats and utilize posts for boat mooring. In this situation, two _____ _____ can be easily "looped" over the top of the post to secure the boat.

Nylon lines are deteriorated by: **dry rot**; **salt water**; or **exposure to the sun**.

The bowline, "the king of nautical knots," typically should not be utilized as shown above, because it cannot be undone under _____.

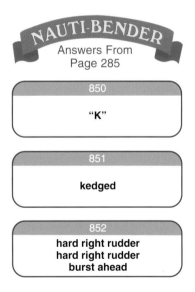

NAUTI-BENDER

Answers From
Page 285

850

"K"

851

kedged

852

hard right rudder
hard right rudder
burst ahead

859

PHOTO: COURTESY OF BERTRAM YACHTS

Running into a big headsea, your boat begins to pound heavily and the bow begins to stuff into each succeeding wave. In this situation, what corrective maneuver is advisable?

860

Turn on a Dime (Heavy Seas): Place engine(s) in neutral; turn the wheel hard over. When the boat begins to lose momentum, goose the engine(s) ahead full throttle to complete the turn... **what is the next step**?

NAUTI-BENDER
Answers From
Page 286

853

capsizing

854

clove hitch
half hitch

855

A: standing part
B: bitter end   C: bight
hank = 100 feet

861

PHOTO: COURTESY OF FORMULA BOATS, BY TODD MARTENS

Jackrabbit Starts Save Fuel: If you throttle up to two-thirds of maximum power as soon as possible, a gasoline engine pumps the optimum fuel/air mix into the cylinders – **True** or **False**?

When underway ahead, increasing speed tends to move the pivot point farther **astern** or **forward**?

Staying "on course", without a "snake wake", is best achieved by **making slight course corrections...** or **large course corrections and then returning the rudder to amidships before reaching the desired heading**.

Whether a vessel has a diesel or gasoline engine, it is always good practice when starting it, to check the exhaust to ensure _____ _____ is coming out.

You're cruising 20 miles offshore. You observe a yellow flare off your starboard bow... what does this indicate?

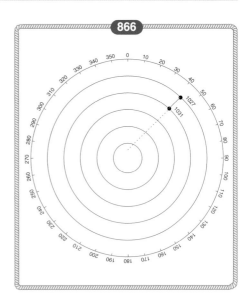

Radar Plotting: For any given speed, the distance in yards traveled in three minutes is 100 times the speed; e.g., a vessel making _____ knots will cover 1,000 yards in three minutes.

NAUTI-BENDER
Answers From Page 288

859

reduce speed

860

throttle back to neutral; center the wheel; accelerate to full throttle

861

True
(Studies have shown a fuel savings of up to 15%.)

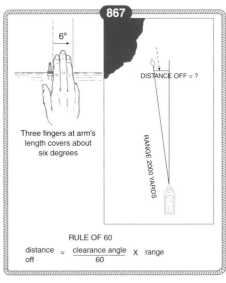

The "rule of 60" equates that an angle of six degrees will give a clearance of 1/10 the range. In the above example, if you steered six degrees to the right of the direct bearing to the buoy, what would the distance off be?

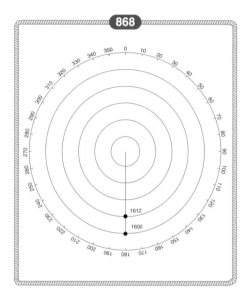

868

You're under way at five knots and note a radar contact ten miles directly astern. Twelve minutes later the contact is directly astern at eight miles... what is the contact's speed?

869

How Much Time Before the Sun Sets (middle latitudes): Hold out your hand (horizontally) at arm's length, determine how many fingers the sun is above the horizon... each finger equals approximately _____ minutes.

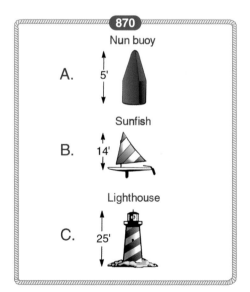

870

Nun buoy

A. 5'

Sunfish

B. 14'

Lighthouse

C. 25'

With clear visibility, at what approximate distance (¼ **nm**, ½ **nm**, **1 nm**, **2 nm**, or **4 nm**) can the objects "**A**", "**B**", and "**C**" shown above be seen and recognized at sea?

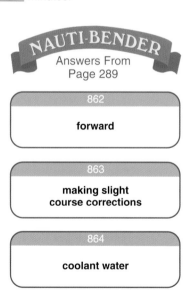

NAUTI-BENDER
Answers From
Page 289

862

forward

863

making slight course corrections

864

coolant water

What term is used to describe doing a task on a boat in a slipshod or sloppy manner?

The zip-out vinyl windows on a flybridge enclosure are often referred to as "_____".

NAUTI-BENDER
Answers From
Page 290

865

A submarine is approaching the surface.

866

1/100 X 1000 = 10 knots

867

200 yards

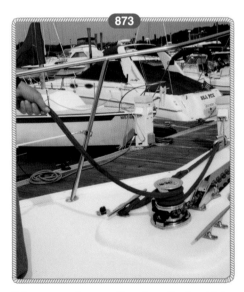

When you "_____" a line, it should be "surged" while maintaining a strain, without parting.

Old salts sometimes refer to the: **harbor pilot**; **radio speaker**; **lower steering station**; or **the auto pilot** as "Iron Mike".

PHOTO: COURTESY OF HATTERAS YACHTS

The power actually available (after the losses in the engine, shaft, and propeller slip) to move a boat through the water, is referred to as: *indicated horsepower*, *shaft horsepower*, or *effective horsepower*.

Inveterate sailors sometimes refer to the auxiliary engine as the "iron _____", "gasoline _____", and/or the "diesel _____".

Frequently used short-term docks (public landings, gas docks, etc.) sometimes utilize a "rail system" to facilitate tying-up various _____ boats. What is an excellent knot to use for this application?

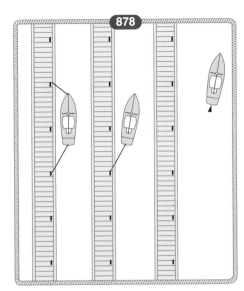

The above unberthing procedure (assuming no current) would be proper with the wind coming from _____ _____ _____.

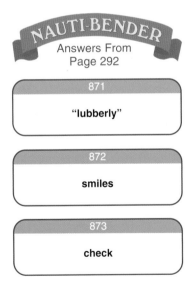

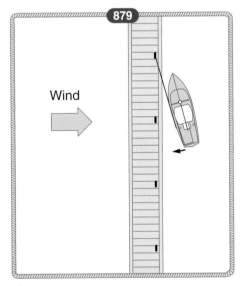

In the above spring-line docking scenario, the engine should be in **forward** or **reverse** and the rudder hard **right** or **left**.

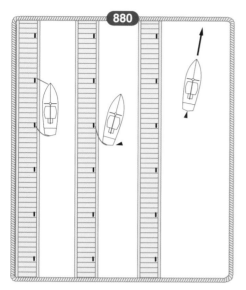

The unberthing procedure shown above would be proper with the wind and current coming from **ahead** or **astern**.

You launch the boat at a nearby lake. When docking at the town dock, you note that the First Mate (he/she) must have forgotten to stow the fenders on board. Using your problem-solving abilities you substitute with a _____ _____ PFD.

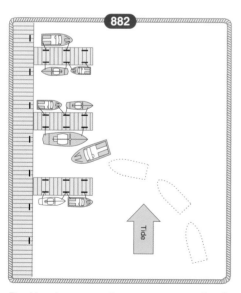

Docking in a normal manner at an unfamiliar marina, you sense the approach is not working (as shown above)... what should you do next: **take aggressive corrective action**; **alert the crew to fend off**; or **back down and try it again**.

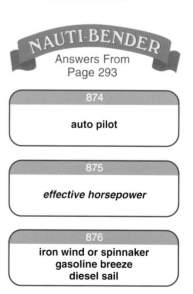

NAUTI-BENDER
Answers From
Page 293

874

auto pilot

875

effective horsepower

876

iron wind or spinnaker
gasoline breeze
diesel sail

883

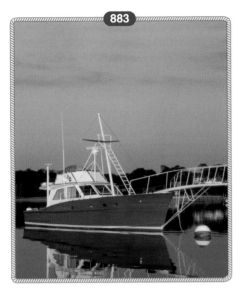

Meticulous seamen keep their vessels in *bristol fashion* by not overlooking the smallest details; e.g., the screws holding fixtures should be aligned: square shape – slots in the _____ direction; circular – slots lie parallel with the _____.

884

PHOTO: COURTESY OF BOSTON WHALER BOATS

Does your outboard idle fine but bog down under load? Many times this malady is caused by a cracked or displaced O-ring at the gas tank or the engine. To check, squeeze the _____ _____ as you throttle up.

NAUTI-BENDER
Answers From
Page 294

877
various length boats **clove hitch**

878
from off the dock

879
engine: **in reverse** rudder: **hard left**

885

PHOTO: COURTESY OF BERTRAM YACHTS

TEN CORROSION KILLERS
1. Inspect and replace zinc anodes regularly.
2. Wash down the boat after each use.
3. Drain the bilges after each use.
4. Use silicone spray on exposed wires.
5. Seal wiring harness feed-throughs.
6. Keep metal accessories and parts waxed.
7. Neutralize battery acid spillage.
8. Lubricate snaps and fasteners often.
9. Fog engine exteriors regularly.
10. Shrink-wrap boat tightly during storage.

Which of the above "corrosion killers" is **incorrect**?

Painting Tip: When applying bottom paint, if you should get some on your skin, don't wash it off with: (A) **solvent**; (B) **Acetone**; and/or (C) **denatured alcohol** as it or they will drive poisons further into your skin.

It is not advisable to use dacron sail covers with _____ sails because the dacron will trap condensation and cause the _____ to rot.

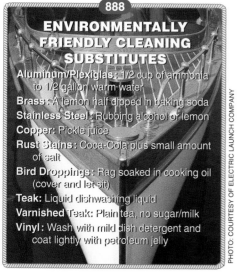

ENVIRONMENTALLY FRIENDLY CLEANING SUBSTITUTES

Aluminum/Plexiglas: 1/2 cup of ammonia to 1/2 gallon warm water

Brass: A lemon half dipped in baking soda

Stainless Steel: Rubbing alcohol or lemon

Copper: Pickle juice

Rust Stains: Coca-Cola plus small amount of salt

Bird Droppings: Rag soaked in cooking oil (cover and let sit)

Teak: Liquid dishwashing liquid

Varnished Teak: Plain tea, no sugar/milk

Vinyl: Wash with mild dish detergent and coat lightly with petroleum jelly

PHOTO: COURTESY OF ELECTRIC LAUNCH COMPANY

Which of the above inexpensive, home-made cleaning substitutes is incorrect?

NAUTI-BENDER
Answers From
Page 295

880

wind and current from ahead

881

seat cushion PFD (Caution: compression reduces PFDs' floatability characteristics.)

882

back down and try it again

One-third Fuel Rule: One-third out, one-third in, and one-third in _____ .

Caution is required when passing through bridges in strong current conditions. **Don'ts include**: starting through before bridge is _____ open; sailing through; following too closely; or going through simultaneously with oncoming boats.

Answers From
Page 296

883

square: **the same direction**
circular or oval:
parallel with the perimeter

884

primer bulb
(The engine will speed up.)

885

10: Minimal ventilation will increase corrosion caused by condensation or residual moisture.

You're cruising at full throttle (or "hooked-up", as the old salts would say) in a vessel that is powered by a 150 HP outboard... approximately how many gallons-per-hour is the engine consuming?

892

PHOTO: COURTESY OF GRADY-WHITE BOATS

893

PHOTO: COURTESY OF TRACKER MARINE L.L.C., BY MIKE FULLER

Conserving Fuel: Keep a minimum of gear and fuel on board... only bring what you need. Run gasoline engines at between _____ to _____ rpm and diesel engine(s) at **one-half**, **two-thirds**, or **three-quarters throttle**.

Assume your Bassboat is skimming over the water at 40 MPH and you momentarily let go of the steering wheel... what will the boat probably do?

894

The bridge is finally opening and a strong tidal current is running... which line of boats: the **up-bound** or the **down-bound** should proceed first?

Answers From
Page 297

886

all of the above
(Use traditional hand cleaners.)

887

cotton
cotton

888

Aluminum/Plexiglas: Ammonia will pit aluminum and may cloud Plexiglas.

Working together to keep our waters clean... in U.S. territorial waters you must be at least _____ miles offshore before raw sewage may be discharged from a vessel.

Many collisions occur on the edge of fog; therefore, the rule: "sound signals must be sounded _____ or _____ an area of restricted visibility."

NAUTI-BENDER
Answers From
Page 298

889
reserve

890
fully open

891
15 gallons (rule-of-thumb): $\frac{\text{Eng. HP}}{10}$ = approx gal/hr. used

After filling the cooler with pan fish at your favorite lake, you decide to trailer the boat to a nearby river to do some trout fishing. Before departing you should inspect and remove the _____ _____ from your trailer and propeller.

When approaching a fog bank, the boat's speed must be reduced so it may be stopped within **25%**, **50%** or **100%** of the visibility distance?

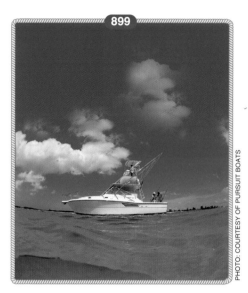

How many miles offshore must you be to legally discharge garbage (bottles, cans, food waste, etc.) overboard: **3**, **6**, **12**, or **25** nautical miles?

PHOTO: COURTESY OF PURSUIT BOATS

While under sail, you find yourself on a collision course with a commercial fishing vessel engaged in fishing. Which boat is the "stand-on" or privileged vessel?

NAUTI-BENDER

Answers From
Page 299

892

**3,000 to 3,500 rpm
three-quarters throttle**

893

**An immediate right-hand turn
and might eject
the passengers.**

894

**Narrow Channel Rules...
the down-bound boats
should go first.**

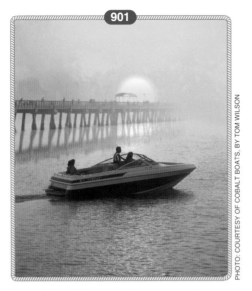

PHOTO: COURTESY OF COBALT BOATS, BY TOM WILSON

Red skies during evening hours indicate a
_____ forecast.

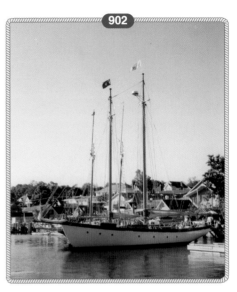

A telltale attached to a shroud on a docked
boat will indicate the **true** or **apparent** wind
direction.

PHOTO: COURTESY OF HYDRA-SPORTS BOATS

The color of the sky is a good weather predictor: **red in the morning** – _____ weather; **gray in the morning** – _____ weather;
pale yellow at sunset usually means –
_____ weather.

Even on the hottest day, the wind chill factor will keep you cooler on-the-water. For example, on a 90° F, dead calm day... if you were cruising at 20 mph... **what would the the air temperature feel like to you**?

Cloudy Weather Forecaster: High clouds, 18,000 ft and above... a change within _____ hours; medium clouds, 6,500 to 18,000 ft... a change within _____to _____ hours; low clouds 6,500 ft and below... you're already in the soup!

NAUTI-BENDER
Answers From
Page 301

898
50%

899
12 nautical miles
(Please help keep
our waters clean.)

900
the fishing boat
(rule: engaged in fishing)

The tide *turns* approximately every _____ hours.

Flag Etiquette: At morning colors, the ensign is hoisted _____, before other flags. At evening colors, the ensign is lowered _____, with ceremony, after all other flags.

Although your yacht club may not approve, the _____ prevention system, shown above, is 99% effective (excluding fly-bys). Lash wind socks or pieces thereof to a length of "small stuff" and string it fore and aft.

NAUTI-BENDER
Answers From
Page 302

901
fair forecast
("Red skies at night...
sailors' delight".)

902

true

903
**bad weather
fine weather
rainy weather**

PHOTO: COURTESY OF HATTERAS YACHTS

With a boat having a planing hull, a 10% increase in horsepower will increase its top speed about 5%. However, a 10% increase in weight will decrease its top speed by **5**, **10**, or **20%**.

A vessel is said to have been "_____" when a following sea overtakes her and breaks over the stern.

When offshore, and conditions make it almost impossible for even the Coast Guard to maintain headway, it is time to "_____ _____".

After a distress call, the radio signal indicating that you may resume normal radio operation is "_____ _____".

NAUTI-BENDER

Answers From
Page 303

904

60° F
1.5 X 20 mph = 30° - 90° = 60°F

905

a change within 24 hours
a change within 6 to 12 hours

906

six hours

Answers From
Page 304

907

rapidly
slowly

908

seagull prevention system

909

5% decrease in top speed (One should consider this when loading up the boat.)

Answers From
Page 305

910

pooped

911

time to heave to

912

seelonce feenee

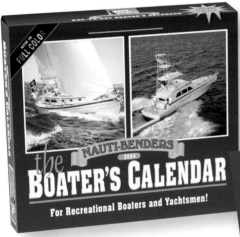

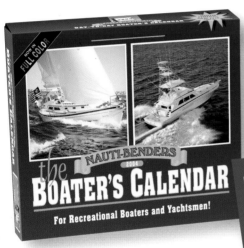
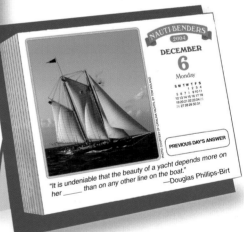